D1487263

PHONOGRAPH

Sound on Disk

These and other books are included in the Encyclopedia of Discovery and Invention series:

Airplanes	Movies
Anesthetics	Phonograph
Animation	Photography
Atoms	Plate Tectonics
Clocks	Printing Press
Computers	Radar
Genetics	Railroads
Germs	Ships
Gravity	Telephones
Human Origins	Telescopes
Lasers	Television
Microscopes	Vaccines

PHONOGRAPH
Sound on Disk

by BRADLEY STEFFENS

The ENCYCLOPEDIA of
D·I·S·C·O·V·E·R·Y
and **INVENTION**

P.O. Box 289011 SAN DIEGO, CA 92198-9011

For James Malone,
who pointed the way.

Library of Congress Cataloging-in-Publication Data

Steffens, Bradley, 1956-
  Phonograph: sound on disk / by Bradley Steffens.

    p. cm.—(The Encyclopedia of discovery and invention)
  Includes bibliographical references and index.
  Summary: Traces the history of the phonograph, from the
early days of the gramophone, to electrical recording, to
stereo and digital sound.
  ISBN 1-56006-222-3 (acid-free paper)
  1. Phonograph—Juvenile literature. 2. Sound—Recording
and reproducing—Juvenile literature. [1. Phonograph—
History. 2. Sound—Recording and reproducing—History.]
I. Series.
TS2301.P3S73 1992
621.389'3'09—dc20   92-27850
                                                  CIP
                                                  AC

Contents

■■■

Foreword 7

Introduction 10

CHAPTER 1 ■ The Signature of Sound 12

Léon Scott invents the phonautograph;
Finding a way to make the phonautograph talk;
A fruitless search for support.

CHAPTER 2 ■ Talking Machine 18

An accidental discovery;
Puzzling delays;
Spurred to action;
Thomas Edison builds and tests the first phonograph.

CHAPTER 3 ■ Phonograph Versus Graphophone 26

From dictation to talking dolls;
The invention of the groove and floating stylus;
Edison introduces his "perfected" phonograph;
A startling announcement.

CHAPTER 4 ■ A New Industry 39

Coin-operated entertainment;
Consumers buy phonographs for home use;
Sousa's marches sing;
Disks replace cylinders.

CHAPTER 5 ■ Electric Recording 50

The first electric recording;
Bell Telephone Company patents first all-electric
    phonograph;
RCA Victor introduces "long playing" records;
The War of the Speeds.

CHAPTER 6 ■ Revolutions   58
    Records on the airwaves;
    "Gold records" for sales of one million;
    The payola scandal rocks the recording industry;
    Recorded music opens new worlds.

CHAPTER 7 ■ Stereo   68
    Two-channel recording on tape;
    Record companies put two channels of sound
        into one groove;
    Stereophonic phonographs are introduced;
    Stereo recordings become popular.

CHAPTER 8 ■ Digital Sound   75
    Computers and digital recordings;
    The first optical disk storage system;
    The compact disc arrives.

    Glossary   87
    For Further Reading   89
    Works Consulted   90
    Index   91
    About the Author   95
    Picture Credits   96

Foreword

The belief in progress has been one of the dominant forces in Western Civilization from the Scientific Revolution of the seventeenth century to the present. Embodied in the idea of progress is the conviction that each generation will be better off than the one that preceded it. Eventually, all peoples will benefit from and share in this better world. R.R. Palmer, in his *History of the Modern World*, calls this belief in progress "a kind of nonreligious faith that the conditions of human life" will continually improve as time goes on.

For over a thousand years prior to the seventeenth century, science had progressed little. Inquiry was largely discouraged, and experimentation, almost nonexistent. As a result, science became regressive and discovery was ignored. Benjamin Farrington, a historian of science, characterized it this way: "Science had failed to become a real force in the life of society. Instead there had arisen a conception of science as a cycle of liberal studies for a privileged minority. Science ceased to be a means of transforming the conditions of life." In short, had this intellectual climate continued, humanity's future would have been little more than a clone of its past.

Fortunately, these circumstances were not destined to last. By the seventeenth and eighteenth centuries, Western society was undergoing radical and favorable changes. And the changes that occurred gave rise to the notion that progress was a real force urging civilization forward. Surpluses of consumer goods were replacing substandard living conditions in most of Western Europe. Rigid class systems were giving way to social mobility. In nations like France and the United States, the lofty principles of democracy and popular sovereignty were being painted in broad, gilded strokes over the fading canvasses of monarchy and despotism.

But more significant than these social, economic, and political changes, the new age witnessed a rebirth of science. Centuries of scientific stagnation began crumbling before a spirit of scientific inquiry that spawned undreamed of technological advances. And it was the discoveries and inventions of scores of men and women that fueled these new technologies, dramatically increasing the ability of humankind to control nature—and, many believed, eventually to guide it.

It is a truism of science and technology that the results derived from observation and experimentation are not finalities. They are part of a process. Each discovery is but one piece in a continuum bridging past and present and heralding an extraordinary future. The heroic age of the Scientific Revolution was simply a start. It laid a foundation upon which succeeding generations of imaginative thinkers could build. It kindled the belief that progress is possible as long as there were gifted men and women who would respond to society's needs. When Antonie van Leeuwenhoek observed *Animalcules* (little animals) through his high-powered microscope in 1683, the discovery did not end there. Others followed who would call these "little animals" bacteria and, in time, recognize their role in the process of health and disease. Robert Koch, a German bacteriologist and winner of the Nobel Prize in Physiology and Medicine, was one of these men. Koch firmly established that bacteria are responsible for causing infectious diseases. He identified, among others, the causative organisms of anthrax and tuberculosis. Alexander Fleming, another Nobel Laureate, progressed still further in the quest to understand and control bacteria. In 1928, Fleming discovered penicillin, the antibiotic wonder drug. Penicillin, and the generations of antibiotics that succeeded it, have done more to prevent premature death than any other discovery in the history of humankind. And as civilization hastens toward the twenty-first century, most agree that the conquest of van Leeuwenhoek's "little animals" will continue.

The *Encyclopedia of Discovery and Invention* examines those discoveries and inventions that have had a sweeping impact on life and thought in the modern world. Each book explores the ideas that led to the invention or discovery, and, more importantly, how the world changed and continues to change because of it. The series also highlights the people behind the achievements—the unique men and women whose singular genius and rich imagination have altered the lives of everyone. Enhanced by photographs and clearly explained technical drawings, these books are comprehensive examinations of the building blocks of human progress.

PHONOGRAPH

Sound on Disk

PHONOGRAPH

Introduction

"I'm dreaming of a white Christmas."
"He's a real Nowhere Man."
"Kris Kross will make you jump, jump."

Most people recognize at least one of these lines from popular songs. They may be able to hear the tunes and even imagine the voices of the people who made them famous—Bing Crosby, The Beatles, and Kris Kross. These memories result from having heard the songs performed in the same way dozens, sometimes even hundreds, of times. Most people have never heard a live performance of these songs. They have heard them through permanent sound recordings.

The first machine to record and reproduce sound was the phonograph. Since its invention in 1877, the phonograph has gone through many changes. Recordings have been made on various materials—tinfoil, rubber, wax, shellac, vinyl, wire, tape, glass, and aluminum—using many different methods. No matter how the recordings have been made, however, they have always served the same purpose: to preserve sounds that exist for only a brief moment.

Nearly every sound known to humankind has been recorded using some form of phonographic equipment. The voices of great leaders, authors, and poets speak to us across time and space through the miracle of sound record-

▪▪▪ TIMELINE: PHONOGRAPH

1 ▷   2 ▷ 3 ▷   4 ▷ 5 ▷ 6 ▷ 7 ▷ 8 ▷

1 ▪ 1851
Léon Scott records the presence and shape of sound waves.

2 ▪ 1876
Charles Cros describes a method of recording and reproducing sound.

3 ▪ 1877
Thomas Edison builds the first working phonograph.

4 ▪ 1887
Emile Berliner patents a process for making recordings on flat phonographic disks.

5 ▪ 1888
Edison introduces the phonograph as a dictation, taking device.

6 ▪ 1890
Phonographs are used for entertainment for the first time.

7 ▪ 1891
First phonographs for home use are sold.

8 ▪ 1896
Berliner develops shellac compound for making disk records.

9 ▪ 1920
Lionel Guest and H.O. Merriam make the first phonograph recording using electricity.

ings. Performances of operas, plays, and songs—the great and the trivial alike—can be heard over and over. Sound effects, from the clip-clop of horses' hooves to the roar of a jet airplane, have been captured with vivid realism on disk. Sounds made by other species, from the songs of humpback whales to the trill of an oriole, have been recorded for study and pleasure. Through recorded news reports, history speaks with its own voice.

The phonograph has been a boon to education and study as well. The Library of Congress lists more than 700,000 different recordings in its catalog. Vanishing languages, dialects, and folklore have been captured in recordings for study by linguists and anthropologists. Reminis-cences, known as oral histories, have been preserved for future historians.

The phonograph has especially enriched the lives of the blind. In 1931, Congress established a free national library service to provide "talking books." This program provides sound recordings to more than half a million people each year.

Today, many machines bring sounds and pictures into our homes. Even so, devices for producing recorded sound alone continue to be important. They no doubt will remain so as long as people have the desire to hear again and again the words, sounds, and music that inspire and entertain them.

10 ■ 1931
RCA Victor introduces 12-inch long playing records.

11 ■ 1946
Columbia Records introduces 12-inch long playing records made of vinylite that play at 33$^1/_3$ revolutions per minute.

12 ■ 1949
RCA introduces a 7-inch record that plays at 45 revolutions per minute, beginning the War of the Speeds.

13 ■ 1955
Ampex Corporation makes the first two-channel, or stereo, recording on magnetic tape.

14 ■ 1957
A single-groove stereo recording system is developed.

15 ■ 1967
NHK Technical Research builds the first analog-to-digital converter, marking the advent of digital recording.

16 ■ 1978
The Philips company announces the first optical disk recording system.

17 ■ 1982
The first compact disc, or CD, is released.

18 ■ 1992
Sony introduces the pocket-size Mini Disc recording system.

The Signature of Sound

Charles Cros was known throughout nineteenth-century France as an important poet. Like most poets, Cros loved the sound of human speech—consonants, vowels, rhymes, alliteration. He used sound to emphasize the meaning of his poems, to draw attention to certain ideas. Cros also was a keen observer of nature. His poetry was rich with precise descriptions of the physical world.

In addition to his verbal skills, Cros possessed a practical mind. He did not just write about nature, he studied it. He experimented with it. He dabbled in astronomy, mathematics, chemistry, and optics. Most of his work was strictly amateur; he did it for the love of learning. But in 1869, Cros stumbled upon a breakthrough that earned him a measure of fame as a practical inventor. He discovered and published the first workable theory for taking color photographs.

That same year, Cros published a book entitled *Études sur les moyens de communication avec les planètes* ("Studies on the Means of Communication with the Planets") in which he proposed building giant, concave mirrors capable of focusing sunlight onto Venus and Mars. Heat from the mirrors, Cros reasoned, could be used to burn geometric shapes into the surfaces of the planets. These symbols, Cros suggested, would be visible to higher life-forms living in outer space.

Cros's interest in the natural world led him to join the Academy of Sciences in Paris. There, Cros was able to keep up with scientific discoveries around the world. With a poet's passion for sound and the scientist's interest in technology, Cros was deeply impressed by the work of another French scientist, Léon Scott. In 1851, Scott had found a way to make a permanent record of the presence and shape of sound waves. This discovery inspired Cros to dream another big dream. He wanted to build a machine that would reproduce sound.

The Phonautograph

Cros studied Scott's discovery carefully. He found that Scott had begun by building a machine that would mimic the workings of the human ear.

Scott knew that people could hear because the energy of sound waves strikes a thin membrane in the ear, the eardrum, and causes it to vibrate. The vibration of the eardrum causes a series of small bones to move back and forth. One of these bones, known as the stirrup, lies against the spiral-shaped chamber called the cochlea. The motion of the stirrup disturbs the fluid in the cochlea. This action stimulates nerve endings, which creates the sensation of hearing.

To build his machine, Scott started with a flexible disk, known as a diaphragm. Like the eardrum, the diaphragm would vibrate when struck by sound. Scott connected a tiny rod to the

HOW THE EAR FUNCTIONS

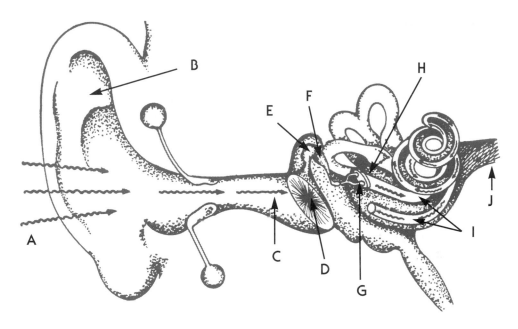

Léon Scott, the first person to record the presence and shape of sound waves, based the design for his recording device, the phonautograph, on the structure and workings of the human ear. Other scientists who experimented with recording or reproducing sound also studied the ear. In fact, when Alexander Graham Bell built his own phonautograph in 1874, he used a real human ear, which he procured from a cadaver.

What interested Scott and Bell about the ear was its natural ability to convert the energy of sound waves into mechanical energy. What impressed Bell, in particular, was the fact that sound waves, acting on the tiny membrane of the eardrum, were strong enough to move the bones of the inner ear. If sound waves carried that much force, Bell reasoned, perhaps their energy could be harnessed to reproduce sound.

The portion of the ear that converts the energy of sound waves into mechanical action is the eardrum, a thin membrane stretched across the ear canal. Sound waves (A) collected by the contours of the outer ear (B) are funneled into the ear canal (C), so they strike the surface of the eardrum (D). The force of the sound waves causes the eardrum to vibrate. The eardrum is connected to a series of small bones known as the hammer (E), anvil (F), and stirrup (G). When the eardrum vibrates, it moves these bones.

One side of the stirrup, known as the oval window (H), lies against a spiral-shaped chamber called the cochlea (I). The cochlea is filled with fluid and lined with 25,000 hairlike nerve endings. When the stirrup moves, it disturbs the fluid in the cochlea. The motion of the fluid stimulates the nerve endings. The nerves send impulses to the brain via the auditory nerve (J). These impulses cause the sensation known as hearing.

center of the diaphragm. Like the bones of the human ear, the rod would move back and forth when sound waves struck the diaphragm. At the end of the rod, Scott affixed a small brush. Under the brush, Scott placed a piece of paper blackened with carbon soot from an oil lamp.

To test his device, Scott sat in front of the diaphragm and spoke in its direction. At the same time, he moved the paper beneath the brush. As sound waves from Scott's mouth struck the diaphragm, it vibrated, causing the rod and brush to move back and forth. The bristles of the brush swept across the moving paper, scraping bits of soot off the paper. This action made a white, wavy line on the paper. When Scott stopped speaking, the diaphragm stopped moving, and the line on the pa-

Léon Scott's phonautograph was the first device to record the shape of sound waves. This 1866 model etched the record of sound waves onto paper wrapped around a hand-cranked cylinder.

per straightened. When he spoke again, the diaphragm, rod, and bristles once again jumped, again creating a wavy line. Scott was the first person in history to see what a sound wave looked like.

When the sounds were high-pitched, Scott noticed, the waves on the paper were packed close together. When the sounds were low-pitched, the waves on the paper were long, spread out. Loud sounds etched big waves. Soft sounds etched small ones. Each separate sound wave left its own unique signature on the page. Scott called his device for recording the shape of sound waves the phonautograph. The name came from the Greek words *phonos*, meaning "sound," *auto*, meaning "self," and *graphos*, meaning "write."

Scott's findings allowed scientists to study sound more closely than ever before. For the first time, sound waves could be measured and compared with precision.

Reversing the Process

Charles Cros believed the phonautograph could do more than simply further the understanding of sound. He reasoned that its workings could be used to create a machine never dreamed of before—a machine to reproduce sound.

Cros based his thinking on the insights of Alexander Graham Bell. "If the motions indicated by the curves [of the phonautograph] could be produced mechanically in any way, the sounds would be audible," Bell stated in various lectures during the 1860s. Bell himself could not think of a way of doing this. In 1876, Charles Cros did.

graph was attached to the diaphragm, Cros reasoned, any movement of the brush would cause a movement of the diaphragm. Cros needed to find a way to move the brush along the path it had traced across the recording surface.

Cros's solution was amazingly simple. He pictured replacing the soft brush with a sharp, hard point, or stylus. Cros imagined the stylus moving not across a flat surface, but rather following along the bottom of a deep groove—a groove that matched the back-and-forth tracings of the phonautograph. As the stylus traveled between the walls of the groove, it would move side to side. The motion of the stylus would cause the diaphragm, in turn, to move in and out. The in-and-out motion of the diaphragm would produce sound.

Engraved Disks

To make a groove, Cros drew upon his knowledge of photography. He knew that light causes certain chemicals to change. For example, light causes an acid-resisting chemical known as potassium bichromate to dissolve. Since 1839, this knowledge had been used to engrave metal plates for printing. To do this, printers coated a metal plate with potassium bichromate and exposed it to light. The plate was then placed into an acid bath. Where the potassium bichromate had not dissolved, the chemical repelled the acid, leaving the metal surface intact. Where light had caused the potassium bichromate to dissolve, however, the acid ate into the metal plate, making a line or groove. Since the placement of the

Alexander Graham Bell knew what needed to be done to reproduce sound but not how to build the machine that would accomplish this task.

The key to making the phonautograph talk, Cros knew, was to cause its diaphragm to vibrate according to the pattern inscribed on the blackened paper. Since the brush of the phonauto-

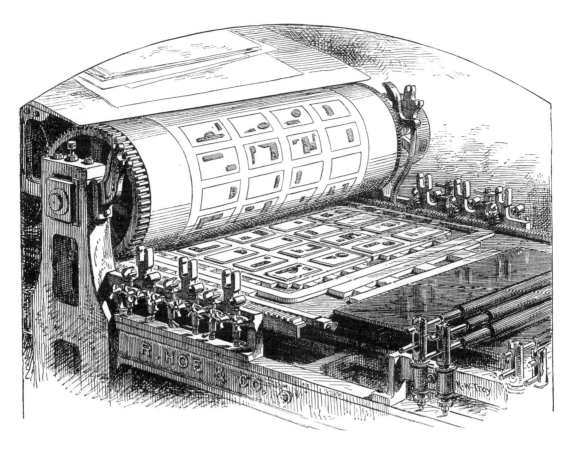

Photoengraving, which uses light to dissolve chemicals on a metal plate, had been used to make printing plates since its invention in 1839. Charles Cros planned to use the process to engrave the tracings of a phonautograph into a metal plate.

groove in the metal plate was caused by exposure to light, this process became known as photoengraving.

Cros reasoned that he could use this method to engrave the tracings of a phonautograph into a metal plate. Cros planned to place a sheet of paper bearing the tracings of a phonautograph on top of a plate coated with light-sensitive chemicals. He would then expose the plate to light. The light would shine through the white lines of the phonautograph, causing the chemicals beneath to dissolve. Meanwhile, the chemicals beneath the black portions of the paper would not change at all. Cros would

then place the plate into an acid bath. Where the chemical had been dissolved, the acid would eat into the metal plate, making a small depression, or groove. This groove would match the tracings of the phonautograph exactly.

To record long periods of sound—an entire spoken poem, for instance, or a piece of music—Cros knew he would need a long, continuous groove. To make such a groove, Cros planned to have the phonautograph trace its line onto a disk that would revolve as the recording was made. The phonautograph arm would move inward from the edge of the disk, causing the brush to trace a long, spiral-shaped line. This line would then be photoengraved onto a metal disk.

To produce sound from the recording, Cros would place the stylus at the beginning of the photoengraved groove and turn the disk. Since the stylus would retrace its path exactly, Cros reasoned, the vibrations it would impart to the diaphragm would match those of the original phonautograph exactly.

Cros wrote down his idea and illustrated it with simple drawings. On April 16, 1877, Cros's paper, entitled "Process for Recording and Reproducing Those Phenomena Perceived by the Ear," was published. Two weeks later, on April 30, the Academy of Sciences in Paris accepted Cros's paper and registered it. This was proof that Cros was the first person to devise a method of recording and reproducing sound.

Seeking Support

Certain that his device would work, Cros set about to build it. Although he could furnish a blueprint for his design, Cros did not have the tools or knowledge to build a working model. He needed to hire a skilled machinist, someone with a working knowledge of metal and mechanics. This required more money than Cros could spare, so he sought a business partner.

Throughout the summer of 1877, Cros approached a number of wealthy businesspeople, asking them to invest in his project. No one was interested. At the same time that Cros was seeking support for his idea, Alexander Graham Bell was trying to find backers to form telephone companies in countries around the world. Some investors reasoned that the future of communications was in Bell's device, not Cros's. Others took a wait-and-see approach. Perhaps someone else would come up with a device that was better than Cros's, they thought. They did not want to sink their money into an invention that might become obsolete in a few months or years.

As Cros traveled from one disappointing meeting to another, important news came from America. Someone had built a talking machine. That man was Thomas Alva Edison.

Talking Machine

Thomas Edison had achieved fame long before he developed the first working phonograph. In 1870, at the age of twenty-three, Edison made major improvements in the stock ticker, a machine that relayed stock exchange prices over telegraph lines. Western Union, the world's largest telegraph company, paid the young inventor thirty thousand dollars for the right to use his patent.

In 1875, Edison built a large, barn-like building in Menlo Park, New Jersey, that held an office, a library, a laboratory, and a machine shop. Edison planned to devote himself full-time to inventing. He hired several workers to help him build and patent his inventions. One of these workers was John Kruesi, a machinist. It was his job to build working models of the devices Edison described in his notes and sketches. Another of the workers was Charles Batchelor, a draftsman. Batche-

Thomas Edison was already well known by the time he invented the phonograph.
One of his inventions, the stock ticker, relayed stock prices to the New York City stock
exchange (pictured) and to other exchanges.

Edison (below) was hard at work on another invention when he accidentally discovered the principle behind the phonograph. Much of his work was done in his Menlo Park, New Jersey, laboratory, illustrated above.

lor turned Edison's rough sketches into drawings that would be accepted by the U.S. Patent Office in Washington, D.C.

An Accidental Discovery

Edison was widely known for his slow, methodical approach to inventing. The process of inventing was not sudden, Edison said. It required many hours of careful, patient work. He described the process as "one percent inspiration and ninety-nine percent perspiration." This description may have been true for many of the more than one thousand inventions Edison patented, but it was not the case for one of Edison's most famous inventions—the phonograph. In fact, Edison's first encounter with the

principle behind the phonograph was accidental.

At the time he discovered a way of recording and reproducing sound, Edison was not working on the phonograph at all. He was building a device that would automatically repeat a telegraph message sent in Morse code:

> I was engaged upon a machine intended to repeat Morse characters, which were recorded on paper by indentations that transferred their message to another circuit automatically, when passed under a tracing point connected with a circuit closing apparatus.

As he was working on July 18, 1877, Edison slid a piece of the indented paper beneath the telegraph. The wire end of a small spring attached to the telegraph happened to be resting on the indented paper as Edison moved it. Edison heard a strange sound. He later wrote:

> In manipulating this paper, I found that when the indented paper was turned with great swiftness, it gave off a humming noise from the indentations, a musical rhythmic sound resembling that of human talk heard indistinctly.

A Faint Hum

This faint hum set Edison's mind whirring. For almost a year, Edison had been working on improvements in the telephone. Each working day had been filled with thoughts about sound and vibrations. Edison knew that a moving diaphragm could produce sounds as complex as human speech. Edison realized that if he could force a diaphragm to vibrate according to a pattern indented in some material, the diaphragm would emit sounds that matched the pattern.

If the pattern in the material was made by a diaphragm responding to sound waves, Edison reasoned, then the diaphragm would emit sounds that matched the original sound waves. Such a machine, Edison guessed, would not only record sound waves, as Léon Scott's phonautograph did, but it would also reproduce them. The machine would talk.

Recording Speech

Edison found a diaphragm he had used in his telephone experiments and affixed an embossing, or indenting, point to its center. He then fitted the diaphragm to his telegraph machine so the embossing point just barely touched a piece of paraffin, or waxed, paper. Even before he tried out his device, Edison was sure it would work:

> I saw at once that the problem of registering human speech so that it could be repeated by mechanical means as often as might be desired, was solved.

With Charles Batchelor looking on, Edison slid the paper beneath the embossing point as he shouted "Hello." Edison noted the result in his notebook:

> Just tried experiment with a diaphragm having an embossing point held against paraffin paper moving rapidly[.] The Spkg [speaking] vibrations are indented nicely and there's no doubt that I shall be able to store up and reproduce automatically at any future time the human voice perfectly[.]

Despite his apparent excitement, Edison did nothing about his invention for almost a month. Then, on August 12, 1877, Edison made another drawing

"A Highly Bold and Original Idea"

By November, Edison still had done nothing with the phonograph. Then something strange happened. On November 17, 1877, one of Edison's associates, Edward H. Johnson, wrote a letter to the important science magazine *Scientific American* describing Edison's phonograph.

> Mr. Edison in the course of a series of extended experiments in the production of his speaking telegraph, lately perfected, conceived the highly bold and original idea of recording the human voice upon a strip of paper, from which at any subsequent time it might be automatically re-delivered with all the vocal characteristics of the original speaker accurately reproduced. A speech delivered in to the mouthpiece of this apparatus may fifty years hence— long after the original speaker is dead— be reproduced audibly to an audience.

Some scholars suggest Johnson wrote this letter to spur Edison to action. Other scholars believe Edison had already decided to work on the phonograph and that he urged Johnson to write the letter announcing it. Either way, twelve days later Edison drew a sketch of the machine he wanted John Kruesi to build.

In his new design, Edison replaced the strip of paper with a piece of tinfoil. The foil was placed around a grooved cylinder. The cylinder was mounted on a feed screw, which was connected to a hand crank. As the crank was turned, the feed screw turned the cylinder. As it turned, the screw moved the cylinder past a stationary stylus connected to a diaphragm. When the diaphragm vi-

Charles Batchelor, the draftsman Edison hired to work in his laboratory, was present when Edison first tried to use the power of sound waves to indent paraffin paper.

of his new device. This time, he drew two embossing points, one for recording sound waves and one for playing them back. This was to be the basic structure of Edison's phonograph when he decided to build it. But that was still some months off.

It is not clear why Edison took so long to build his first phonograph. Perhaps because the discovery was accidental, Edison did not value it as much as he might have had he been hired to invent a device for recording sound. The discovery was, in a sense, an interruption. Edison's goal was to perfect his device for repeating telegraph messages, and his work on that device was not yet complete. Little did he realize that the phonograph would bring him millions of dollars more than he would ever earn from his improvements in the telegraph.

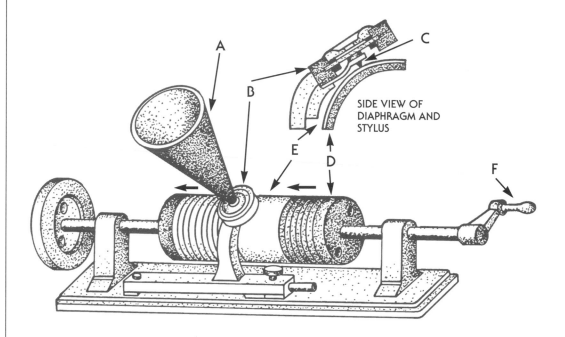

SIDE VIEW OF DIAPHRAGM AND STYLUS

Thomas Edison's phonograph was the first device to record sound waves and generate sound. Edison succeeded where others had failed by converting energy from sound waves into three-dimensional recordings. These three-dimensional recordings allowed Edison to not only record sound but also reproduce it.

The phonograph's cone-shaped mouthpiece (A) directs sound waves toward a small, metal diaphragm (B). A steel stylus (C) is attached to the diaphragm. The force of the sound waves vibrates the diaphragm, which in turn moves the stylus up and down. Beneath the stylus is a grooved brass cylinder (D) covered with a sheet of tin foil (E). The up-and-down motion of the stylus indents the foil. A hand crank (F) rotates the cylinder and moves it horizontally from one side of the phonograph to the other. As the cylinder moves, the indentations form a long spiral pattern along the grooves.

To play the recording, the listener returns the cylinder to its original position, places the stylus against the indented tin foil, and turns the cylinder again. The dents in the tin foil cause the stylus to rise and fall exactly as it did when the dents were made. The up-and-down motion of the stylus causes the diaphragm to vibrate, producing audible sounds. These sounds match the sounds that formed the indentations.

brated, the stylus indented the tinfoil to varying depths. Another stylus and diaphragm were attached to the opposite side of the cylinder from the indenting stylus. The second diaphragm, designed to reproduce the sounds from the indentations, was thinner than the first diaphragm, so it moved more easily.

On December 1, 1877, John Kruesi returned to Edison with the completed machine. Edison checked the position of the recording stylus and diaphragm. Then he tried the crank. Everything was just as he had sketched it.

Edison wrapped a sheet of foil around the cylinder. Then he adjusted the recording stylus so it barely touched the foil. Slowly he turned the crank. At the same moment, he lowered his lips to the diaphragm and began to shout "Mary Had a Little Lamb." When he finished reciting the nursery rhyme, Edison raised the stylus off the foil and cranked the cylinder back to the starting position. He then placed the playback stylus at the beginning of the tiny row of dimples indented by the recording stylus. Once more, he turned the crank. The playback stylus moved up and down with the indentations in the tinfoil, causing the attached diaphragm to vibrate. Edison's voice—scratchy but distinct—filled the room.

Complete Success

"I was never so taken aback in my life," he later stated, recalling the success of the experiment. "I was always afraid of things that worked the first time."

Over the next few days, Edison demonstrated his new invention to his friends and associates. Everyone marveled to hear their own voices mysteriously arise from the shiny paper. On

Edison's first phonograph made a three-dimensional replica of sound waves by indenting tinfoil. In this photograph, the foil on the left side of the cylinder has been indented, while the foil on the right side remains smooth.

December 7, 1877, Edward H. Johnson telegraphed another associate of Edison, Uriah H. Painter, about the new device:

> Phonograph delivered to me today. Complete success. Talks plainer than the telephone.

The editors of *Scientific American* had been intrigued by Johnson's letter of November 17, so Johnson and Edison demonstrated the working device for them. An account of this meeting was published in the December 22 issue of the magazine:

> Mr. Thomas Edison recently came into this office, placed a little machine on our desk, turned a crank, and the machine inquired as to our health, asked how we liked the phonograph, informed us that *it* was very well, and bid us a cordial good night. These remarks were not only perfectly audible to ourselves, but to a dozen or more persons gathered around, and they were produced by the aid of no other mechanism than the simple little contrivance explained and illustrated below.

The account was followed by Johnson's letter and a sketch of the device. Edison's breakthrough instantly became famous.

To the Patent Office

It was unusual for Thomas Edison to discuss an invention before securing a patent for it. He did not want other inventors to copy his ideas before he had gained sole legal right to use them. But in the case of the phonograph, which, because of its accidental discovery, was already different from his other inventions, Edison had made an exception to

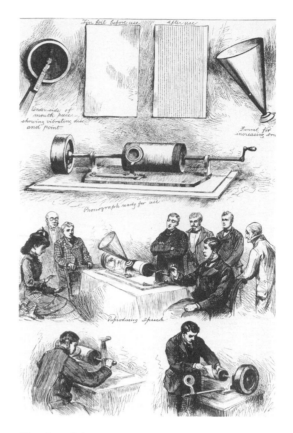

Sketches of the phonograph in action, from the March 30, 1878, issue of Harper's Weekly.

his rule. Once the details of the device appeared in the pages of *Scientific American*, however, Edison rushed to the patent office to register his device.

Charles Cros did not contest Edison's patent application. It is doubtful that Cros could have blocked the patent, since Edison's method of recording differed from Cros's method in one important way. Cros's method used a back-and-forth, or lateral, motion within a groove to record the impression of sound waves. Edison's method used vertical, or hill-and-dale, motion across a flat surface to achieve the same result.

On January 30, 1878, the U.S. Patent Office granted a patent to Thomas Edison for the invention of the phono-

*"I was never so taken aback in my life,"
Thomas Edison said of the success of his first experiment with the phonograph. The young inventor is shown here with one of his earliest working models.*

graph. This patent gave Edison the sole right to build talking machines in the United States.

With his new device protected by patent, Edison built several models to demonstrate its powers. On March 11, 1878, Edison's representatives took one of these models to the Academy of Sciences in Paris. Among those in the audience was Charles Cros.

The poet and inventor listened carefully as the workings of Edison's machine were described in detail. Then, less than a year after he had registered his own plans for building a phonograph, Charles Cros heard Edison's machine talk. Cros was thrilled. The man who had dreamed of building the first talking machine rose to address the assembly. He called the new device a great breakthrough and hailed its inventor as a man of genius.

Phonograph Versus Graphophone

Inventing a device was one thing. Making money with it was quite another. No one knew this better than Thomas Alva Edison, one of the world's first full-time inventors. Edison usually sold his patents to others, letting them tend to the business of making money with his ideas. But Edison's plans for the phonograph were different. He decided to build and market the talking machines himself.

Because the invention of the phonograph was accidental, Edison faced an unusual problem. He was not sure who

would want to buy it. Most of the time, Edison invented things for other people who knew what they were looking for and how they would use it. No one was paying Edison to invent a phonograph, however. It just happened. And Edison was not quite sure what to do with it.

He had plenty of ideas, though. He wrote down several for a magazine article that appeared in *Harper's Weekly* on March 30, 1878. He ranked the uses in what he believed to be their order of importance:

True to his 1878 prediction, Thomas Edison designed and built a talking doll that held a small phonograph inside. The doll's owner could make short recordings on a wax cylinder that came with the phonograph (right).

1. letter writing and dictation
2. talking books for the blind
3. the teaching of elocution
4. reproducing music
5. the "Family Record," preserving sayings and memories of family members and recording the last words of the dying
6. talking dolls and other toys
7. speaking clocks
8. preserving languages by reproducing the pronunciation exactly
9. preserving spoken explanations by teachers for future reference by pupils
10. connecting up with the telephone to make permanent records of communications

The list shows uncommon foresight, even for a practical genius like Edison. Except for speaking clocks, each use on the list would one day become commonplace. Some, such as music reproduction, would become big businesses. Others, such as the teaching of elocu-tion and the preservation of languages, did not grow into big businesses, but they did become common practices within specialized fields. Even talking dolls, such as Mattel's Chatty Cathy, which used small disk recordings, re-sulted from Edison's breakthrough.

Novel Uses

Edison was not the only person to think of new uses for the device he had invented. Among those drawn to the device was Alexander Graham Bell. As a teacher of the deaf and the inventor of the telephone, Bell spent his career thinking about and experimenting with sound. In fact, Bell briefly thought of challenging Edison's patent for the phonograph on the basis that he had thought of the concept first. "It is a most

Alexander Graham Bell (top row, far right) in a portrait of faculty and students from Pemberton Avenue School for the Deaf in Boston, Massachusetts. As a teacher of the deaf, Bell thought often about sound.

astonishing thing to me that I could possibly have let this invention slip through my fingers when I consider how my thoughts have been directed to this subject for so many years," Bell wrote to his father-in-law and business partner, Gardiner Hubbard, after reading a detailed description of the phonograph. Bell planned to use his lecture notes about reversing the action of the phonautograph to prove that he had conceived of the principle of the phonograph first. "So nearly did I come to the idea that I had stated again and again in my lectures the fundamental principles of the phonograph," wrote Bell.

Bell's father-in-law and his lawyers convinced him not to attempt to block Edison's patent, however. They argued that if Bell's statements about the phonautograph were said to be enough to block Edison's patent, then the statements made by others prior to Bell's invention of the telephone might be used to take away Bell's most important

Bell considered challenging Edison's phonograph patent but dropped this idea when he realized it might fuel challenges to the patent for his telephone (pictured).

patent. Several inventors, backed by Western Union, were already suing Bell over his telephone patent. Bell decided to drop his challenge over the phonograph.

Bell clearly was excited by Edison's discovery, though. He thought of novel uses for the new device. One was a type of alarm that would work like a ratchet noisemaker. A stylus and diaphragm attached to the ratchet would be placed inside a sounding chamber along with a strip of indented tinfoil. As the sounding chamber spun around the ratchet, the tiny phonograph inside would cry "help!" or "fire!" In the spring of 1878, Bell wrote to Gardiner Hubbard that such a device would allow them to "realize a large fortune in a couple of months or so."

A Child's Toy

It was never clear why Bell thought a person would rather use this device rather than simply shout "fire!" or "help!" One of Bell's biographers, Robert V. Bruce, suggested that Bell thought of it because of his lifelong work with deaf people who could not always speak—or shout—clearly. In any event, the alarm idea went no further than the letter to Gardiner Hubbard.

Bell called his second idea the "swearing top." It was a novelty item that Bell thought could be sold as a Christmas toy. He planned to wrap a tinfoil recording of some startling words or phrases around a spinning top. To make the toy cry out, a child would touch the recorded strip with a stylus connected to a diaphragm. Bell wrote to his associate, Thomas Watson, telling him to build such a device right

The cover of Frank Leslie's Illustrated Newspaper, *April 20, 1878, shows a woman using an Edison tinfoil phonograph. This phonograph has a large flywheel on one end to help the user maintain a steady cranking speed.*

away. Bell saw another fortune in the near future. With the money from the swearing top, Bell wrote to Watson, "we can work at Flying Machines & all sorts of things next year in comfort."

Watson immediately foresaw problems with the device. He wrote back to Bell that a spinning top "could hardly speak the shortest word before it made several revolutions." Since he was hard at work improving the telephone, Watson did not believe he should take time to solve the many technical problems of a toy. Bell gave up the scheme, though not his interest in the phonograph itself.

The Edison Speaking Phonograph Company

On April 24, 1878, Thomas Edison formed the Edison Speaking Phonograph Company in the United States.

On the same day, his representatives filed for a British patent covering refinements Edison had made in his phonograph. The new model had a much longer cylinder than the original device did, so it would produce recordings of greater length. Edison added a heavy flywheel to one end of the cylinder. The momentum of the turning flywheel helped the user maintain a steady cranking speed. Edison replaced the two diaphragms—one for making the recording and one for playing it back—with a single diaphragm that performed both functions. He added a large cone, or megaphone, to focus sound waves toward the diaphragm when recording and to amplify the sounds during playback. Edison would devote no more time to the phonograph for the next ten years.

His reason for stopping work on the phonograph was not that it was perfect.

It was not. It did not record sibilant sounds—those made by the letters "c," "s," and "x"—very well at all. Some vowel sounds were hard to tell apart. Alexander Ellis, an associate of Alexander Graham Bell, reported, "The extreme vowel sounds *ee* and *oo* were scarcely differentiated."

The reason Edison abandoned the phonograph was that in November 1878 he signed a contract that required him to devote all of his time for the next five years to developing an electric light.

"It Talks. It Whispers. It Sings."

Edison sold the rights to his talking machine to a group of investors, one of whom was Gardiner Hubbard. Edison was paid ten thousand dollars and was guaranteed a 20 percent royalty for each phonograph sold. By 1879, the Edison Speaking Phonograph Company was offering phonographs to the public for ten dollars, a considerable sum at the time. "It Talks. It Whispers. It Sings," announced one advertisement for the new machine. A few people purchased the early Edison models, but most were disappointed in the results. The tinfoil recordings were not very clear, and they wore out quickly. Sales fell off, and in June 1880, the Edison Speaking Phonograph Company suspended business.

Although Thomas Edison was not free to work on the phonograph, other scientists, including Alexander Graham Bell, were. Using ten thousand dollars in prize money awarded to him in 1880 by the French government for his work on the telephone, Bell founded a research laboratory like Edison's to pursue new inventions. Bell called the new

laboratory the Volta Laboratory after the award he had received, the Volta Prize. Bell's cousin, Chichester Bell, and a hired assistant named Charles Sumner Tainter joined Bell in the venture.

When they formed the Volta Laboratory, the Bells and Tainter agreed that each inventor would receive credit for his own inventions. To ensure that proper credit was given, the partners promised to keep careful notes. Each agreed to not "claim as his own, ideas that had not been reduced to writing," as Bell put it. "We were all provided

Charles Sumner Tainter conceived the idea of cutting a groove into a recording surface. The groove produced less distortion and clearer sound than did Edison's indenting method.

with scribbling-books and our claims to invention were to stand or fall by our written notes."

Tainter's Breakthrough

On March 28, 1881, Tainter used his scribbling-book to jot down an idea for the phonograph that would lead to the most valuable single patent ever produced by the Volta Laboratory. Tainter's idea was to cut a groove into the recording cylinder instead of merely indenting it.

The difference was small but important. Edison's indenting stylus simply displaced material on the recording surface, like a finger pushing into a lump of clay. Each time the stylus formed a dimple, it disturbed the surrounding material. Some of this material bordered the last dimple formed by the stylus. As a result, the shape of the previous dimple changed. When the shape of the dimple changed, the sound it produced changed, too. In other words, each impression distorted the one before it.

With Tainter's method, the stylus shaved material off the recording surface, like the tip of a knife etching a line into clay. The stylus still moved up and down, but it chiseled its way through the material like a knife, rather than punching its way along like a finger. The cutting action kept the stylus from disturbing the material around it, so there was less distortion during the recording.

Tainter was not the first to think of using a groove in sound recordings, of course. Charles Cros had conceived and published the same idea three years before. When Cros heard Edison's phonograph play, however, he gave up on his own effort to build a similar device. Had he pursued his concept, Cros would have found that he had underestimated the difficulty of photoengraving a steel disk with the line traced by a phonautograph. Tainter, on the other hand, realized that the recording surface should be made of something soft and easy to carve. Wax seemed ideal.

A Summer of Experiments

Throughout the summer of 1881, the members of the Volta Laboratory worked at refining Tainter's breakthrough. They tried to leave impressions on the recording surface both by cutting into it and by adding material to it. Later, Tainter described the process this way:

> We made many experiments with etching records and also with electroplating or building up of the record. . . . Different shaped cutting styles and those not adapted to cutting were tried. Much time was devoted to electrotyping, moulding, and copying of records. Records were made by means of photography, and by sensitive jets of liquids. We experimented with stearine, stearine and wax, stearine and paraffin, wax and oil. . . .We made records by jets of semifluid substances deposited on the recording surface, also records on narrow strips of paper, disks, and tubes, with many forms of machines for using wax-coated disks and cylinders, with many forms of recorders and reproducers for wax-coated cylinders.

Among the methods tried in Washington that summer was the lateral cut process first described by Charles Cros. The Bells and Tainter called this the "zig-zag" approach. One thing they liked about this method was that the

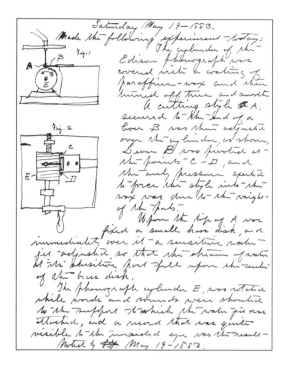

A page from Charles Sumner Tainter's 1883 notebooks shows one of the many experiments he conducted to improve the phonograph.

recordings through the constant friction of a stylus passing over the record surface. In one method, they used a common telephone diaphragm to vary the current through a wire to an electromagnet. The electromagnet altered the surface of a metal record, creating a magnetic recording path. A magnetized stylus then traced along the magnetic path without touching it. They also devised a stylus that emitted a jet of air as it followed along a groove in the recording surface. This last process worked fairly well, and the partners built a working model of it.

Another Breakthrough

In the fall of 1881, the Bells and Tainter placed notes of their experiments and a working model of the air jet phonograph, which they called the graphophone, in a sealed box. They took this box to the Smithsonian Institution and left it with the curators of the museum. This action allowed the inventors to establish the date of their inventions without making their breakthroughs known to the public through the patent process. If other inventors later tried to patent devices like theirs, the Volta partners could block the patent by proving that they had invented the device first.

Through the winter of 1881-82, the members of the Volta Laboratory, especially Chichester Bell and Tainter, worked at perfecting the phonograph. Then, in February 1882, Tainter had another brilliant idea. He reasoned that since the deep record groove had walls on each side, the pickup stylus could follow along the recorded track on its own, without being held in place by a screw. Tainter devised a flexible, or floating,

walls of the groove strictly controlled the motion of the stylus in two directions, left and right. With the hill-and-dale method, the stylus was controlled in only one direction—down. Nothing controlled the stylus as it rode up over indentations in the record. Although the zig-zag design was in some ways better than the hill-and-dale design, the Volta partners had a hard time making it work. The playback, or pickup, stylus they used was too heavy to move back and forth easily. After testing the zig-zag method for several months, they returned to the hill-and-dale approach.

An interesting aspect of the partners' work that summer was what Tainter called "various methods of reproducing sounds without contact with the record." Tainter and his partners wanted to avoid wearing down the pickup stylus to ride between the walls of the groove. The lightweight stylus glided over the hills and dales at the bottom of the groove with much less friction than the standard stylus did.

Since the lightweight pickup moved up and down easily, it responded to even the smallest undulations in the record's surface. As a result, it produced more and clearer sound than the fixed stylus. It also produced less wear on the recording than did the fixed pickup. The lighter pickup allowed for a smaller stylus, which meant the grooves could be cut finer. Narrower grooves meant more grooves could be cut on each wax cylinder, extending the playing time of the recording.

The Volta Graphophone Company

Again, the members of the Volta Laboratory placed their notes and device in a sealed box and deposited it with the Smithsonian Institution. For two more years, the partners continued to work on the phonograph. Finally, on June 27, 1885, the Bells and Tainter applied for five patents covering their methods, ideas, and devices. All five patents were granted on May 4, 1886.

Even though Charles Sumner Tainter had thought of the incised groove by himself, lawyers for the Volta Laboratory applied for the patent covering this vital breakthrough—Patent Number 341,214—in the names of both Tainter and Chichester Bell. Tainter was stunned. He later came to believe that the lawyers had placed the Bell name on the patent because "it improved the outlook from the businessman's standpoint. The justice of the matter did not trouble them." Tainter did not fight the decision, however, since the three partners had agreed to share all profits from Volta Laboratory patents regardless of whose names appeared on them.

On the same day that the patents

The graphophone, produced by the Volta Graphophone Company, included a long, narrow cylinder coated with wax. A sharp stylus cut a groove into the wax surface.

were granted, Alexander Graham Bell, Chichester Bell, and Sumner Tainter formed the Volta Graphophone Company in Alexandria, Virginia. The goal was to sell the improved talking machine to business owners and court reporters as a dictation-taking device. Their machine was powered by a foot treadle, like those used to power sewing machines. It came with a set of listening tubes, like those of a stethoscope.

In 1887, a group of court reporters and other investors approached the Volta Graphophone partners with a plan to invest in the new device. The investors offered to trade shares in a new phonograph company, which they called the American Graphophone Company, for the important phonograph patents. The Bells and Tainter agreed. They accepted the shares, turning over the day-to-day business of selling talking machines to others.

An 1898 Sears catalog advertisement (above) offers the graphophone, "the Greatest and Most Wonderful of Inventions." (Below) The graphophone records (left) and talks (right) in an 1889 illustration.

A close-up drawing of an 1897 French phonograph shows a stylus incising the recording surface of a cylinder.

The Perfected Phonograph

Thomas Edison was surprised and upset when he heard about the progress made by the Bell-Tainter group. Although he praised their work in public, Edison privately called his rivals "a bunch of pirates." He bought back the shares he had sold in the Edison Speaking Phonograph Company and went back to work on his ten-year-old invention.

It is hard to understand why Edison was angry at the members of the Volta Laboratory. It is true that the Bells and Tainter were trying to make money with an invention Edison had conceived first, but this was not unusual. In fact, Edison had done the same thing to Bell. At the very moment Edison was expressing his contempt for the Bells and Tainter, the greatest portion of his in-

come still came from patents he held for improvements in Bell's invention, the telephone.

Even though Edison was upset that Bell and Tainter had copied his ideas, one of the first things he did was copy two of theirs. He incised a groove into a wax surface just as Tainter had, and he began to use a floating pickup stylus.

Instead of recording on a cardboard cylinder coated with wax, as Bell and Tainter had, Edison devised a cylinder of solid wax. Unlike the cardboard cylinder, the solid wax core could be erased and reused. The user simply shaved off the outer surface of the recording cylinder with a sharp tool, leaving a smooth surface that could be incised again. Edison believed this feature would help him sell his machine to court reporters and stenographers. He was right. In fact, the

Edison uses his own invention, the dictaphone (left). The dictaphone led to an improved phonograph, but its entertainment value was unimagined until a salesman rigged up a device that allowed people to listen to recordings by inserting a nickel into a slot connected to a phonograph (below).

solid wax core dictation machine, or dictaphone, remained in use for nearly one hundred years.

Over the next few months, Edison obtained seventeen patents covering improvements in the phonograph. One of his most important improvements was to rotate the cylinder with a battery-powered motor rather than with a hand crank. In June 1888, Edison believed he had taken his research as far as he could at that time. He offered what he considered his "perfected" phonograph for sale.

Joining Forces

When Edison entered the market with his improved talking machine, there was little demand for the product. Few people understood the new-fangled ma-

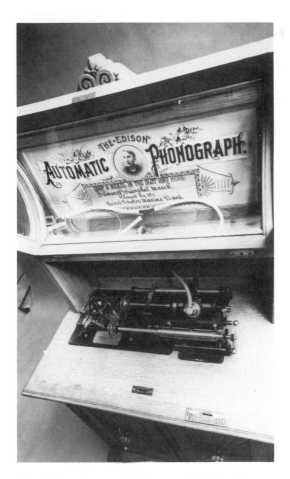

The Edison Automatic Phonograph. The sign reads, "Drop a Nickel in the Slot and Hear Gilmore's Triumphal March played by the United States Marine Band."

Phonograph Company and the American Graphophone Company with a plan. He proposed that the companies join forces to offer both companies' machines for sale together. Instead of competing in a cutthroat manner, the two companies would cooperate, allowing buyers to choose the machine they preferred.

Buyers Make Their Preference Known

On June 28, 1888, an agreement was reached between the Edison Speaking Phonograph Company and the American Graphophone Company for joint sales through the North American Phonograph Company. The sales representatives who worked for Lippincott would be allowed to offer both machines to prospective clients. The plan was to sell the phonographs to businesses, such as law firms, that had a need for taking dictation. To gain the rights to sell the graphophone, Lippincott agreed to buy five thousand of the machines a year from the American Graphophone Company.

Two years after signing the contract, Lippincott organized the first national convention of the North American Phonograph Company. Sales representatives from across the country met in Chicago to discuss the new business. When they added up their combined sales and rentals, they found that buyers preferred the Edison machine fifty-to-one over the Bell-Tainter model. Edison's improvements produced better sound, and the battery-powered motor made it easier to use. Even so, sales of both machines were sluggish. The sales force called for the inventors to create

chine or envisioned how it could help them. To make matters worse, they had to choose between two brands of machine, each associated with a great inventor. One of the first people to grasp the problems facing the phonograph companies was a businessman named Jesse Lippincott. He believed the two great phonograph companies should work together to enlarge the market rather than compete for the few customers who were interested in the device.

In June 1888, Jesse Lippincott approached both the Edison Speaking

more sensitive machines, since buyers of the devices still had to shout into the speaking cone to make an impression on the record.

An Important Use

As the sales representatives discussed ways to improve sales of the talking machine, one of them, Louis Glass of the Pacific Coast Phonograph Company, made a rather startling announcement. Glass disclosed that nearly all the profits he had earned in the past year had come from rentals of the phonograph for entertainment rather than business purposes. Glass had rigged up a device that allowed people to listen to recordings of music and humorous stories by inserting a nickel into a slot connected to a phonograph. Glass rented these coin-operated machines to the owners of saloons and arcades. The renters collected enough nickels from the machines to pay for the rentals and make a handsome profit besides.

Although no one realized it at the time, Glass's statement was destined to change the direction of the phonograph industry forever. From that day forward, those involved with the making and selling of phonographs began to focus more of their attention on the entertainment business. One year later, when Lippincott sponsored a second national sales convention, the sales representatives reported that fully a third of the existing talking machines had been fitted with coin slots and were being used as amusements. Although the use of sound recording for dictation would continue in one form or another up to the present, the real future of the phonograph was in music.

A New Industry

At the second national convention of the North American Phonograph Company, held in New York City in 1891, many sales representatives called upon the parent company to provide prerecorded cylinders for use in coin-operated machines. This was not the first time Lippincott had received such a request. In fact, such recordings were increasingly in demand, especially from James L. Amden of the Ohio Phonograph Company.

The Birth of the Recording Industry

Amden had hired the Standard Locomotive Works in Cincinnati to build ornate steel housings for his coin-operated phonographs. Like others who rented phonographs for entertainment purposes, Amden hired local singers, musicians, and storytellers to record cylinders for use in his machines. But he needed more and better recordings.

Edison himself heard about the requests being made by Amden and others. He sent representatives to the North American Phonograph convention to announce that he was at work on a method of copying recorded cylinders. Those who heard the announcement greeted it with cheers.

Like Glass's statement one year before, Edison's announcement marked the beginning of a new era for the phonograph. Up to that point, Edison, Bell, Tainter, and nearly everyone else in the phonograph business had focused their efforts on making and selling talking machines. Beginning in

An 1889 drawing shows a man playing a cornet into the speaking cone of a phonograph. Early phonographs worked best when reproducing the sounds of instruments that produced sounds close to the middle range of human hearing, such as the cornet.

1891, they began to look closely at the business of making and selling recordings to play in the machines.

This business differed from the manufacturing and sales of phonographs. It involved finding creative talent to make recordings, choosing material people would pay to hear, making recordings that sounded good, and promoting and distributing the finished products. Slowly, this business grew apart from the business of making phonographs. It even came to have its own name, which it bears today—the recording industry. Its product was not machines, but creative works. Its business was show business.

Edison's pre-recorded cylinders were packaged in decorative cardboard tubes (above). The 1907 Edison Home Phonograph (right) came with a cabinet that had room for one hundred cylinders.

Home Entertainment

The new industry received another boost in June 1891. The Columbia Phonograph Company, which handled sales of phonographs in and around Washington, D.C., offered phonographs for sale not just to businesses, but to the public at large. For the first time, phonographs were being used in the home. This was a turning point not only for the phonograph, but for society as well.

The typical American family in 1891 did not own any machine for home entertainment. Radios did not exist. Neither did motion pictures. Television was more than thirty years away from being invented and fifty years away from widespread use. So, for the most part, people provided their own entertainment. Family members played musical instruments, sang together, read aloud from books, put on skits, or played games. When people wanted to be entertained by someone else, they went to a concert or a play. The phonograph changed that. Other devices would follow, but the phonograph was the first to bring professional entertainment into the home.

The First Recording Star

People liked being able to listen to talented performers—musicians, singers, comics—without leaving the comfort of their homes. Thanks to the phonograph, they were able to hear not only the best performers in their area, but also sometimes the best in the world.

The first popular recording artist was the American composer and bandleader John Philip Sousa. Sousa was known as the March King because he had composed hundreds of popular marches, including "Stars and Stripes Forever," "Washington Post," and "Semper Fidelis." In 1891, Sousa was the director of the U.S. Marine Corps Band in Washington, D.C. Over the course of twelve months, Sousa's band made more than 230 records. Most sold out quickly.

Sousa's records were popular for several reasons. His brisk, peppy music appealed to a wide range of people. Also, he was famous before the advent of the phonograph. Many cities and towns had marching bands, and most marching bands played Sousa's work. The phonograph gave people the chance to hear the famous composer's music more often. Finally, and perhaps

The March King, John Philip Sousa, composed and arranged short, peppy tunes that reproduced well on the phonograph.

John Philip Sousa and the Marine Corps Band was the most popular recording ensemble in the 1890s. Although the performing band included more than forty musicians, only about twelve played on the early acoustic recordings.

most importantly, Sousa's music sounded good on the phonograph.

This was not true of all music. The phonograph still did not pick up extremely high-pitched or low-pitched sounds very well. Stringed instruments, such as the violin and viola, did not sound good. Neither did deep basses. Instruments that produced sounds close to the middle range of human hearing came across more clearly. Trumpets, cornets, trombones, French horns, clarinets, oboes, flutes, and even piccolos sounded great. These were the instruments Sousa featured.

The pace of Sousa's music also helped. His short, staccato notes reproduced plainly on the phonograph. Long, drawn-out notes tended to quaver in and out of tune.

The size of the group making a record had to be kept small, again for technical reasons. The cone that gathered the sound for the recording picked up only sounds made directly into it. If a musician stood too far away from the cone, his or her music was lost. For this reason, large orchestras did not record well. Sousa's band was made up of only twelve players. Shoulder to shoulder, they crowded around the recording cone and blew vigorously into their instruments. The tiny diaphragm at the bottom of the cone jumped and fluttered, forcing the recording stylus deep into the wax. No one had to strain to hear a John Philip Sousa record!

The limited range of sound produced by the Edison and Bell-Tainter phonographs was well known to other inventors, many of whom tried to improve the device. One of these inventors was Emile Berliner.

An Old Idea Gains New Life

This was not the first time Edison, Bell, and Berliner had crossed paths. Like Edison and Bell, Berliner had worked on the telephone. Around 1878, Berliner turned his attention to the phonograph. He acquainted himself with the patents of Edison and the Bell-Tainter group, but he also studied the work of Léon Scott and Charles Cros. Berliner was especially interested in Cros's lateral cut method of engraving the recording surface. Like Bell and Tainter, Berliner saw that the lateral cut would control the stylus in two directions throughout recording and playing cycles, rather than in just one. Such control would produce better sound, Berliner reasoned.

Berliner was intrigued by another facet of Cros's design as well—the flat disk. Berliner could see that recorded disks would be more compact and easier to store than the bulky cylinders pioneered by Edison and the Bell-Tainter group. This would not be an advantage in the dictation business, since a disk could not be shaved down and reused as the solid wax core was. But it could be an advantage with prerecorded music, especially for the home market.

Emile Berliner invented the first practical disk records and a machine to play them, the gramophone.

The Berliner gramophone featured a moveable pick-up stylus that traveled from the outer edge of the disk to its center.

This, Berliner believed, was the field in which the recording industry would grow most quickly.

Mass Production

The flat disk offered another even more important advantage, as Berliner saw it. It would be easier to copy than a cylinder was. Copying a cylinder required a tube-shaped mold, which was filled with hot wax. When the wax cooled, it contracted, so it could be slipped from the mold. Although slight, the shrinkage of the recorded surface did distort its sound. The wax cylinders also were fragile and prone to damage when taken from the mold.

A disk, on the other hand, could simply be stamped on one side. It did not have to be heated much to accept an impression. As a result, it would not shrink as much, resulting in truer sound. Since the material used for the disk did not have to be poured into a mold, it was more durable than the wax used for cylinders.

All of these advantages convinced Berliner to try recording on a flat surface. At first he attempted to photoengrave a metal disk as Charles Cros had described in his papers. Cros's method worked, but the resulting sound was not very good. Berliner settled on a simpler method.

Instead of using light to dissolve the coating on a metal plate, Berliner scratched the coating away with a sharp metal stylus. As in Léon Scott's phonautograph, Berliner's stylus was connected to a diaphragm that vibrated when struck by sound waves. As in Cros's disk design, the stylus began at the outer edge of the disk and moved inward, toward the center, as the disk turned. This created a long, spiralling line in the coating on the disk. Berliner then placed the disk in an acid bath. The acid ate into the metal along the line scratched into the coating, creating a spiral groove in the metal disk.

Once Berliner had engraved a master recording, he used it as a mold to make a second metal disk. The metal from the second disk filled the grooves of the master recording, forming a reverse copy of the original—a flat disk covered with a tiny spiralling ridge, instead of a groove. Berliner then used this embossed copy to stamp the surface of another softened rubber disk, recreating the original groove.

The Gramophone

Berliner patented his process in 1887. He gave a public demonstration of his device on May 18, 1888, at the Franklin Institute in Philadelphia. An account of the event appeared in the *Journal of the Franklin Institute*, bringing Berliner instant fame. In 1892, Berliner formed the U.S. Gramophone Company. He designed a hand-cranked phonograph to play his rubber disks and to offer them for sale for home use. The public snatched up the new devices.

Thomas Edison was not impressed with Berliner's gramophone, and he did not consider it a threat to his own phonograph business. Berliner's design was flawed, Edison believed, because the centrifugal force of the spinning disk constantly pushed the floating stylus outward while the spiral shape of the groove constantly pulled the stylus inward. The clash of these opposing forces placed greater pressure on one side of the stylus than on the other. This pressure partly offset the added control of the lateral cut motion, so the reproduction of the sound was not perfect. It also placed greater friction on the outer

wall of the groove than on the inner wall. As a result, the outer wall wore down faster than the inner wall, which distorted the sound.

The sideways motion of the stylus across Berliner's disk created another problem, Edison believed. At the outer edge of the disk, where the groove started, the disk passed under the stylus at one speed, but at the inner edge of the record, where the groove ended, the disk moved under the stylus at a slower speed. This variance in speed across the surface of the record caused distortion in the sound.

Edison's phonograph was free of these distortions because his stylus did not move across the cylinder. The cylinder moved sideways beneath the stylus. As a result, the stylus in Edison's phonograph rode right down the middle of

The May 16, 1896, issue of Scientific American *showed several views of "The Gramophone—The New Talking Machine."*

A list of recordings published by the United States Gramophone Company in January 1895 contains eighty-six titles. A line at the bottom of the page states, "It is expected that between 25 and 50 New Pieces will be added every month."

the groove, so it did not wear down one wall of the groove.

Although Edison was right about all the problems of a lateral cut disk, he exaggerated their importance. The distortions he described were small. The average person could not hear any distortion at all. Berliner's records sounded as good if not better than Edison's. They were also cheaper and easier to handle. It did not take long for sales of the flat disks to surpass those of cylinders.

Even so, Edison clung to his belief that his design was better. He waited until 1913 before he began to produce flat disks and players. Even then, he continued to engrave the records with the vertical hill-and-dale method rather than with a lateral cut. He also continued to release cylinder recordings until 1928.

Quieter Records

As sales of his gramophone climbed, Berliner tried to find a better material than rubber to form his disks. In 1896, he developed a shellac compound that was easy to stamp when warm but turned hard when cool. The glassy surface of the shellac greatly reduced surface noise. It also was less prone to warping than the rubber was. The black shellac disks also played more loudly. The modern record was born.

In 1897, Berliner hired a machinist named Eldridge Johnson to build a spring-powered motor strong enough to power the turntable, the disk that turned the phonograph records. Johnson's new design was much easier to use than the old hand-cranked models. Instead of having to stand by the machine and turn the crank, the owner of the new gramophone simply wound up the spring and tripped a lever. The spring powered the turntable during the entire recording. The listener could just sit back and relax.

The recording industry, born during the era of the cylinder recordings, began to flourish with the coming of disks.

The market for new records exploded. The search for new talent became a big business. The New England Phonograph Company hired an artist named Russell Hunting to record a series of humorous stories featuring a character named Casey. Russell performed with an Irish accent that many people found amusing. Meanwhile, the New Jersey Phonograph Company signed a contract with John Philip Sousa's Grand Concert Band. In New York, a record maker named Gianni Bettini recorded the voices of many famous people reading or simply speaking. One of the people Bettini recorded was the author Samuel Clemens, better known as Mark Twain. Unfortunately, Bettini's recording of Clemens, the only one the great author ever made, was lost.

Although Berliner greatly improved the quality of mass-produced copies of records, he did not do much to change the quality of the original, or master, recordings. His shellac compound hardened too quickly to be used for making masters. Berliner continued to use rubber, which was not as sensitive as the wax pioneered by Sumner Tainter.

Wax Masters

Berliner's associate, Eldridge Johnson, who had formed his own company after a lawsuit forced Berliner out of business in 1900, began work on a process using wax to make master disk recordings. Johnson was preparing to patent his method in December 1901, but another of Berliner's former employees, Joseph W. Jones, beat him to it.

Jones sold his patent to the Columbia Phonograph Company, which had branched out from cylinder recordings to sell disk records. A year later, John-

Frances Densmore of the Smithsonian Institution used the phonograph to preserve many Native American songs.

Ignacy Jan Paderewski was lured into the recording studio by the improved quality of the phonograph.

son's company, the Victor Talking Machine Company, struck a deal with the Columbia Phonograph Company. They agreed to share all their disk record patents. Thanks to this agreement, the two companies would dominate the disk record industry for the next twenty years.

The wax master process greatly improved the quality of disk recordings. For the first time, stringed instruments could be heard clearly. Deep bass sounds boomed from the horn-shaped speaker of the gramophone. The human voice, with its many vowels and consonant sounds, spoke and sang more plainly than ever before.

A Golden Age

The quality of sound produced by wax masters and shellac copies drew new artists to the recording studio. The world's greatest musicians found that the new methods could capture the verve and nuance of their art. The great Russian composer Sergey Rachmaninoff ventured into the studio to record some of his own works for piano. One of the greatest piano virtuosos of all time, Ignacy Jan Paderewski, also made a few precious recordings. Leopold Stokowski, a world-famous conductor, made recordings for the Victor Company in a classical record series Johnson called the Red Seal series.

By far the most famous recording artist of this period was the Italian opera singer Enrico Caruso. For years, the fiery

Leopold Stokowski raised recorded orchestral music to new heights in a series of performances he conducted for the Victor Company.

Enrico Caruso drew this sketch of himself recording for the Victor Company. The brilliant Italian tenor was the most successful recording artist of the acoustic era.

tenor had thrilled audiences throughout Europe with the power and passion of his extraordinary voice. In 1901, Caruso made his first recordings, three cylinders recorded for the Anglo Italian Commerce Company in Milan. A year later, Caruso made seven disk recordings for the International Zonophone Company. In 1902, Fred Gaisberg of the British Berliner Gramophone Company made ten recordings of Caruso. The rights to some of Gaisberg's recordings were purchased by the Victor Company. These were among the first Caruso recordings to be released in the United States.

When Heinrich Conried, the manager of the Metropolitan Opera Company in New York, heard Caruso sing, he was amazed. He immediately sent the twenty-nine-year-old tenor a contract to sing with the Metropolitan Opera for the 1903-04 season. Caruso accepted. According to author James Robert Smart, "This was probably the first time a phonograph was ever responsible for securing a singer a contract."

Caruso's American debut was a huge success. On February 1, 1904, Caruso went to the Victor studios for his first American recording session. The short

playing time of gramophone records—just three to four minutes—kept Caruso from performing complete operas, but he was able to record many famous arias, or songs. These short, electrifying records sold thousands of copies. In fact, Caruso's recording of *Vesti la giubba* ("On with the Motley") from the opera *I Pagliacci* by Ruggiero Leoncavallo became the first recorded piece to sell one million copies. Already famous, Caruso's records made his name a household word. "You sing like Caruso" entered the language as the ultimate praise a singer could receive. He was the world's first recording superstar.

The constellation of great artists that gathered around Columbia and Victor record companies made hundreds of brilliant records from 1903 to 1925. Not only classical musicians, but jazz and popular artists like Bessie Smith and Al Jolson made records of great beauty. This era became known as the golden age of acoustic music, since no electric power was used to record or reproduce the sound. All the electricity in these early recordings came from the performers themselves.

But that was about to change.

Electric Recording

The science of transmitting sounds via electricity continued to develop throughout the early years of the phonographic industry. Hundreds of refinements were made to the telephone and the electrical wires that carried its signal. In 1894, the Italian inventor Guglielmo Marconi discovered a way to transmit sound through the atmosphere using electrically charged radio waves.

Amplified Signals

Radio technology shaped the future of the phonograph in several ways, but the first effects were technical. To convert sound vibrations into electrical signals that could travel a great distance, the radio needed to boost, or amplify, the weak electrical signal emitted from the mouthpiece, or microphone. In 1906, an American inventor named Lee De Forest patented an electrically powered vacuum tube known as the Audion. The Audion enhanced, or amplified, the electric current that came from the microphone.

Likewise, the radio receiver had to boost the faint signals that traveled to it through the air. De Forest's tube performed this task as well. On March 5, 1907, while giving demonstrations of his device in New York City, De Forest wrote in his diary, "My present task (happy one) is to distribute sweet music broadcast over the city and the sea so that even the mariner far out across the

Lee De Forest holds one of his early vacuum tubes, which boosted the power of electric signals.

silent waves may hear the music of his homeland."

The current received by the radio caused a small electromagnet to vary its magnetic field. The changing magnetic field caused a small magnet attached to a diaphragm to move in and out, closer and farther from the electromagnet. The motion of the diaphragm created sound waves much like those that entered the microphone in the first place. This diaphragm was known as a loudspeaker, or simply, a speaker.

Electrically Powered Stylus

Two researchers with the British Gramophone Company, Lionel Guest and H.O. Merriman, reasoned that vacuum tubes could be used to boost a radio signal enough to also power the incising stylus of a phonograph. In 1920, Guest and Merriman tested their invention during a burial service honoring those soldiers who had died in World War I but whose remains were never found or identified. The service was to be broadcast from Westminster Abbey in London. As radio signals from the ancient church reached Guest and Merriman's receiver, the tubes inside the radio boosted the signal as usual. The strengthened current caused the electromagnet to alter its magnetic field. The changing magnetic field caused the recording stylus to pulse back and forth, engraving sound waves from the solemn ceremony onto a wax master disk.

The quality of the recording made by Guest and Merriman was poor, but it proved that electricity could be used to record sounds. Researchers at the Bell Telephone Company began to experiment with methods of using amplifying tubes to boost signals coming from microphones and create clear recordings. In 1924, the Bell Company obtained a patent for the process and assigned it to its affiliate, the Western Electric Company, for development. Western Electric offered the rights to use it to both the Victor and Columbia record companies.

Greater Clarity

The new process changed the recording industry dramatically. For the first time, recording artists did not have to huddle around the sound cone of an acoustic phonograph to be heard. Sitting or standing in a more natural arrangement, a musician simply played in the direction of a microphone placed nearby. The microphone transformed sound waves from the musician's instrument into a variable, or changing, electric current that moved along a wire, through the amplifying tubes, and finally to the electromagnet that con-

De Forest developed the vacuum tube for radios, such as this model from the De Forest Radio Company, but his invention also led to the development of the electric phonograph.

HOW A PHONOGRAPH WORKS

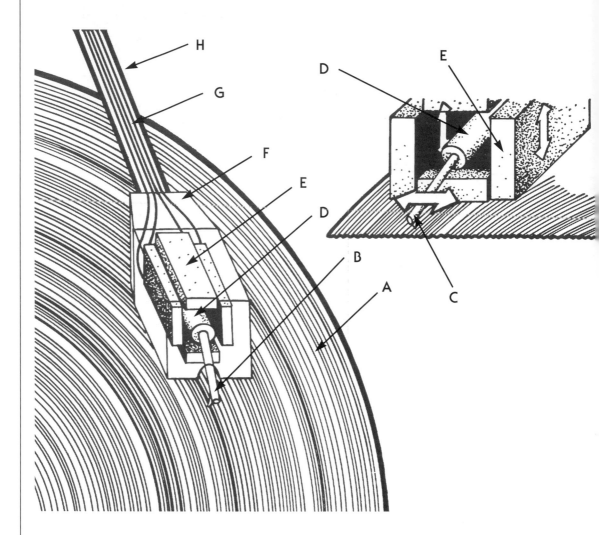

The standard electric phonograph works by converting the three-dimensional impression on the record surface into a variable electric current. This electric signal, boosted by amplifiers, causes the loudspeaker to vibrate, producing sound.

The turntable of a standard phonograph rotates a grooved phonograph disk (A) beneath a stylus (B). The stylus moves from side to side (C) as it follows the contours of the groove. The stylus is attached to a small magnet (D) which moves with the stylus. The magnet is surrounded by coils of wire (E) inside a housing, or cartridge (F). The movement of the magnet within the cartridge strengthens and weakens the electric current flowing through the coils, creating a variable current. This variable current moves through the wires (G) in the pickup arm (H) to the amplifier and, finally, the loudspeaker.

The Victor Salon Orchestra huddles around a large sound-gathering cone during an acoustic recording session (top). Members of the same orchestra later spread out evenly behind a microphone for an electric recording session (bottom).

trolled the recording stylus. By using several microphones, a large group of musicians—an entire orchestra, chorus, or big band—could be recorded clearly.

By boosting the signal from the remote microphones, the electrical recording system captured subtle sounds that the old acoustical system never could. The complex tones of stringed instruments were recorded in all their shimmering beauty. Notes played on string basses, tubas, and timpani were inscribed as distinct tones instead of the muffled rumbling heard on the acoustic gramophone. The sibilant sounds of the human voice hissed into the hot wax.

Electricity made a huge difference in the playback of the recordings as well. Even the tiniest movements of the playback stylus emitted electrical signals that the amplifying tubes could boost into audible sound. The complex tones recorded with the new electrical equipment came through the speakers with startling clarity.

A Trade Secret

Electricity offered another valuable feature to the phonograph: volume control. The gramophone and cylinder phonographs had just one playing volume—"on." The amplifying system of the electric phonograph allowed the electric signal from the stylus to be increased or decreased simply by turning a dial. In 1925,

Columbia and Victor offered electrically recorded disks for sale. The record companies did not promote or even announce the fact that their new records were being made in a new way. They feared that such an announcement might cause the public to stop buying the acoustical recordings that still filled their warehouses from floor to ceiling. The record companies planned to delay their announcement until they had developed an electrical phonograph to play the new disks. In the meantime, the record companies brought their most popular artists back to the recording studio to electrically re-record their most recent records. The companies wanted to have a full catalog of records to offer once electric phonographs were available.

Even without an electrical playback system, the new electrically recorded disks sounded better than the old acoustic ones. Owners of the mechanical gramophone could easily hear the difference. Word about the new disks spread quickly among audiophiles, those who prized quality sound recordings, and they eagerly waited for the giant companies to make their move.

Victor Day

They did not have to wait long. In the fall of 1925, the Victor Company promoted November 2 as "Victor Day," the day the company would release its new electric phonograph, the Orthophonic Victrola. The company sold $20 million worth of the new phonographs in one week.

Between 1925 and 1928, all the other phonograph companies followed Victor into the electric market. Even

Edison's stodgy National Phonograph Company gave in to market pressure. In 1928, the company began releasing electrically recorded disks. At last, Edison gave up on his beloved cylinder process. No cylinders were ever recorded electrically.

Longer Play

The electrical method held another benefit, unseen at first. Because the electrical system could amplify even the smallest vibrations of the pickup stylus, a smaller, even more lightweight stylus could produce clear, loud sound. A

The Orthophonic Victrola featured an automatic record changer so listeners could enjoy an entire symphony or opera without having to change records by hand.

A Columbia Records employee holds a stack of long playing vinyl records that contains the same amount of recorded music as does the pile of 78-rpm shellac records to his right.

smaller stylus meant a record could be made with a smaller groove. A smaller groove meant more grooves—and more playing time—on each side of a record.

Researchers at RCA Victor began experimenting with a smaller groove to create "long playing" records. At the same time, they began testing slower playing speeds. They knew that fast-turning disks made better sound recordings than slow-turning ones because the zig-zag groove made by a sound wave was spread across more of the record surface. The longer groove meant more space to record nuances of the sound wave. But they also knew that the electrically powered turntables spun the records with greater control than the old spring-driven motors, causing less distortion. They believed that the improvement in speed control would more than offset the loss of fidelity that occurred by shifting to a slower recording speed.

In 1931, RCA Victor introduced its new long playing records. The twelve-inch disks were bigger than the old gramophone records, and they held more grooves per inch. These changes alone would have produced longer playing times, but RCA went even further. It cut the playing speed by more than half, from the 78 revolutions per minute (rpm) of the old disks to 33⅓ rpm for the new ones. Playing time more than tripled, from about four minutes for the old 78s to about fifteen minutes for the new long playing disks. For the first time, entire movements of a symphony could be played on a phonograph without a break. RCA introduced a new phonograph designed to play both the old and the new disks.

RCA's breakthrough was fantastic but untimely. In 1931, the United States was in the grip of a worldwide depression. A third of the work force was unemployed. Many of those who did have jobs had lost their savings during a rash of bank closings. Few were willing to spend their income on a new entertainment system.

RCA continued to produce long playing records for five years. Despite the advantages of the new disks, few people bought them. In 1936, RCA abandoned the long playing format. In time, the record giant would return to the format it had pioneered, but only after another company popularized it first.

The Advent of Vinyl

That company was Columbia Records. During the depression and the subsequent World War II, no great advances were made in recording techniques. After the war, however, in June 1948, Columbia held a demonstration of a

As a man and child look on, a worker in a record factory uses a heated press to make a phonograph record. The paper labels stacked on spindles near the worker's left hand are affixed during the record pressing.

new twelve-inch long playing disk. Like the RCA disks, the Columbia disk was made with smaller grooves, called microgrooves, and played at 33⅓ rpm. A major difference existed between the disks, however. The RCA disks were made of the shellac compound developed by Emile Berliner. Columbia made its disks with an unbreakable new substance known as plastic. The special black plastic used to make records was called vinylite, later shortened to vinyl.

Vinyl was cheaper than shellac and easier to stamp with the master disk. As a result, the price of the new records began to fall. More importantly, the new disks produced better sound than the old shellac records. The sleek new surface produced almost no surface noise. The resilient material also was less prone to scratching and nicking, so the disks continued to sound good even after prolonged use.

Columbia was able to squeeze up to twenty-four minutes of playing time onto its long playing disk, which it dubbed and trademarked as the LP. Like RCA's long playing records, the LPs could hold several short songs, entire movements of symphonies, even single acts of operas on one side of a disk.

The LP was an instant success. Every major record company in the country except one switched to the new format. The lone holdout was the company that first developed the LP concept, RCA Victor.

The War of the Speeds

RCA believed it had a better idea. It was at work on a seven-inch disk that played at 45 rpm. Smaller grooves gave the smaller records, known as 45s, greater playing time than the old 78s, though not by much. RCA was not concerned with long playing times. The vast majority of the records it was selling were not long recordings of classical music, but

During the War of the Speeds, record players (right) had to fit three sizes of records and record buyers built up collections in each size: the old 78-rpm shellac records, the 12-inch 33⅓-rpm vinyl LPs, and the 7-inch 45-rpm disks.

duce than LPs, so they cost less to buy. The higher play speed produced slightly truer sound as well. The more compact records were easier to store than LPs and easier to handle. The public, especially younger listeners, loved them.

Phonograph makers were undecided about which side to take in the War of the Speeds. On the one hand, the 33⅓ rpm LPs were very popular, but the 45 rpm disks were selling well, too. In addition, many people still enjoyed listening to their old 78s. Most phonograph makers equipped their machines to play all three speeds.

In 1950, Columbia and Victor struck a compromise. A cross-licensing agreement allowed both companies to issue both LPs and 45s. Furthermore, each company agreed to use the 45 format for popular music and the LP format for classical recordings. At the same time, the 78, the sturdy disk that had served as the foundation of a new industry, was phased out.

short, popular songs by artists like Bing Crosby, Frank Sinatra, Glenn Miller, and others.

RCA introduced its seven-inch disks in 1949, launching what would become known as the War of the Speeds. The small disks were much cheaper to pro-

Revolutions

Technology developed for the radio had a huge impact on the phonograph. Similarly, the growth of the radio as an entertainment medium had an enormous impact on the growth of the record business. The effects of this growth on the art of making music amounted to nothing less than a revolution.

The Effect of Radio

After World War I, radio stations broadcasted entertaining programs free to nearby homes. To make money, the radio stations charged companies money to mention their names and the names of their products during broadcast hours. The companies sponsored certain radio programs and often had brief messages, known as commercials, included in the broadcasts.

To attract listeners, the radio stations had to offer quality programs. In the early years of radio, almost all these programs were performed live. The radio stations hired the foremost entertainers in the industry. All of this high-quality entertainment was free to the listening public. Some people predicted that radio would destroy the phonograph industry. Why, these people asked, would someone buy a record that could be heard for free on radio?

Indeed, record sales fell dramatically with the advent of radio. The only records that sold well were by artists who were not often heard on radio—

black jazz musicians, for example. According to Erik Barnouw, author of *History of Broadcasting in the United States*, the sales of records by these artists saved the record business:

> Sold through separate catalogs—at first, mainly in black ghettos—the records of artists like Bessie Smith continued to have a boom sale. Bessie Smith records apparently kept Columbia Records afloat.

Another form of American music—country-western—had a similar effect on the recording industry. Rarely heard on radio in the 1920s, a few country

Bing Crosby made a name for himself on radio. Radio temporarily slowed the growth of phonograph and record sales.

Country-western artists like "Uncle Dave" Macon (right) and his son, Dorris (left), built up a following through record sales before performing on radio shows like "The Grand Ole Opry."

stars managed to sell many records. Slowly, these artists built up a regional following until they finally began performing on radio too.

Records on the Air

As the national radio networks grew, they used their money and power to attract the top talent in the country to perform live for their audiences. Smaller, local radio stations could not attract the same quality of performers that the networks did. To compete, some radio stations began to play records by the big radio stars. The radio audience enjoyed hearing records on radio, especially new records. More stations began to play records in place of live performances.

Eventually, most local radio stations broadcasted nothing but recorded music interrupted by commercials, news reports, and the brief—often humorous—remarks of the radio announcers. Records became such an important part of the radio format that the radio announcers soon became known as disc jockeys, or simply deejays.

The use of records on radio spurred the growth of the recording and phonograph industries. Radio provided a way for record companies to expose audiences to their new records. Instead of hurting the sales of records, radio actually helped them. The more a record was played on radio, the more people wanted to buy it.

Payola

The record companies slowly realized that radio was not a foe, but a powerful friend. The record companies began a

Radio announcers like Arthur Godfrey became known as disc jockeys because they played popular phonograph records during their broadcasts.

campaign to interest radio stations in their records. Contracts with recording artists required the musicians to give interviews at radio stations or just visit with important deejays. The record companies sponsored radio concerts featuring their artists. Record company executives wined and dined the radio program directors and deejays, hoping a good relationship would ensure that their records would be played.

Some record companies went to even greater lengths to promote their records. They not only pampered the radio executives, they paid them. This practice, known as payola, benefited both radio stations and the record companies. The radio stations made lots of money, and the record companies sold lots of records.

There was a problem, however. The practice was illegal. It broke fair trade laws that had been written to prevent big companies from limiting competition and gaining control of an entire industry.

This was exactly what was happening with payola. Smaller record companies, known as independents, did not have enough money to compete with the large record companies. The small companies found that radio stations would not play their records as often as they played the big companies' records, even though some of their artists were more popular than the artists making records for the big companies.

When the practice of payola became public in the 1950s, it was one of the biggest scandals ever to rock the entertainment industry. As a result, the relationship between record companies and radio stations changed. From that time forward, decisions on which records to play were made on the basis of listener interest, not cash payments.

HOW A RECORD IS MADE

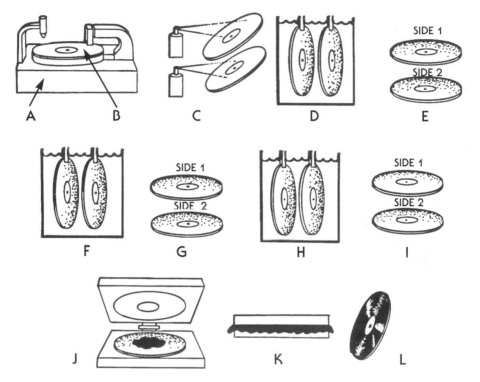

Record-making begins with a tape recording. The tape player sends an electrical signal to a master disk cutter (A). The electrical signal moves the disk cutter's cutting arm from side to side. At the same time, a metal disk coated with acetate, lacquer, plastic, or a combination of all three, rotates beneath the cutting arm. A stylus connected to the cutting arm carves a squiggly line in the disk. This disk is called a lacquer master (B). The lacquer master is removed from the metal plate and coated with silver (C) and placed in a nickel plating bath (D). The nickel fills the grooves of the silver-coated master recording, making a reverse copy of the original with a raised spiral ridge instead of a groove. The reverse copy, known as a master matrix disk (E) is placed in a nickel plating bath (F) to make a second

copy known as a mother matrix disk (G). This copy is an exact (positive) duplicate of the original recording. The mother matrix is then placed in a nickel plating bath (H) to make several stamper dies (I). Each stamper die can be used to stamp out thousands of copies. When one stamper die wears out, another can be made from the mother matrix.

The final step in making a record, requires two stamper dies (one for each side of the record) to be placed face-to-face in a press (J). A piece of softened plastic, known as a biscuit, is placed between the stamper dies. The press closes down on the plastic (K), applying heat and pressure to form a flat disk known as a pressing. The pressing is trimmed to produce the final record (L).

Huge Audiences

Before radio, even the most popular records rarely sold more than 100,000 copies. With the support of radio, records began to sell in the hundreds of thousands, even millions. The first single disk to sell a million copies was Alma Gluck's "Carry Me Back to Old Virginny," released on the Red Seal Victor label. (Sales of Caruso's *Vesti la giubba* totaled more than a million copies, but this was achieved on several different disks made at different recording sessions.)

By the 1940s, million-selling records, though rare, appeared more regularly. The Victor Company (by then known as RCA Victor) honored artists who sold a million records by giving them "gold records." The first such record was spray-painted gold and presented to bandleader Glenn Miller on February 10, 1942, for his recording of "Chattanooga Choo Choo."

A record made four months later, "White Christmas," composed by Irving Berlin and recorded by Bing Crosby on May 29, 1942, became not only a gold record, but also the most popular single recording ever made. On Christmas Eve 1987, it was announced that sales of "White Christmas" had reached 170,884,207 copies in North America alone.

New Security

Such astronomical sales changed not only the recording industry, but the entire field of music as well. Before the phonograph, most musicians eked out a living giving live concerts or performing in revues or musical plays. Most

Popular composer Stephen Foster published several world-renowned songs but never achieved financial success.

gifted songwriters wrote for the musical stage in New York in an area known as Tin Pan Alley. Most songs were sold outright to the producers of the plays and revues. Additional money, if any, came from the sale of published sheet music.

The earnings were meager. For example, Stephen Foster, considered by many to be America's greatest popular composer, published more than two hundred songs between 1844 and 1864. Many of these songs, such as "Oh, Susanna," "Old Folks At Home," "I Dream of Jeannie with the Light Brown Hair," and "Camptown Races," achieved worldwide fame. Despite his songwriting success, Foster had just thirty-eight cents when he died.

The phonograph changed the financial prospects of musicians and composers. Royalties from just one popular record, or hit, could support a recording artist and songwriter for years. For example, the same year Glenn Miller recorded his "Chattanooga Choo Choo," a recording of Foster's "I Dream of Jeannie with the Light Brown Hair" also was released. Enough people bought Foster's song to put it on the Hit Parade, a list of the best-selling records in the United States published by *Billboard* magazine. Although "I Dream of Jeannie" did not become a gold record, it would have been a gold mine for Foster. Had he been alive, Foster would have collected more money from that single record than he earned in an entire lifetime of sheet music royalties and writing for hire.

In earlier times, composers like George Gershwin, Cole Porter, Duke Ellington, Richard Rodgers, and Stephen Sondheim might have scraped along as Stephen Foster did. Thanks to records,

The Beatles, shown here performing on the Ed Sullivan television program, became the most successful recording group of all time, selling more than one billion records worldwide.

Thanks in part to the financial success of her records, jazz artist Billie Holiday was able to rise from humble beginnings to become one of America's greatest performers.

these artists were able to enjoy enough financial security to develop their art.

The chance to gain financial security drew musicians, singers, composers, and lyricists to the field of popular music. Talent that might otherwise have been directed into another field, or not developed at all, blossomed in the recording industry. Songwriters as diverse as blues artist Billie Holiday, country-western singer Hank Williams, and rock-and-roll legend John Lennon rose from humble, even impoverished backgrounds to attain fame and fortune through their records. As a solo artist and as a member of the popular band The Beatles, Lennon sold more than one billion recordings worldwide. Not only his music, but also the thoughts and beliefs expressed in his lyrics enriched the lives of hundreds of millions worldwide.

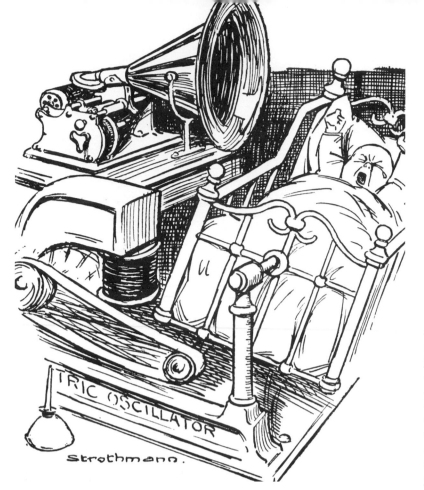

A drawing of a child being sung to sleep by a phonograph illustrates an article entitled "The Menace of Mechanical Music" by John Philip Sousa. The recording industry's first star criticized the growing influence of the phonograph.

The Growth of Classical Music

The effect of the phonograph on classical music was in some ways even more dramatic than the effect on popular music. Before the phonograph, classical music was rarely heard outside large cities, except for works composed for piano or voice. Towns that had concert bands capable of playing the works of John Philip Sousa, for example, rarely had enough people to staff a full orchestra capable of playing a symphony by a classical composer such as Ludwig van Beethoven. Works for orchestras and chamber ensembles were performed mainly at colleges and universities and by a few professional musicians.

Operas were offered only in major cities such as New York, Boston, and San Francisco. The vast majority of classical music was unplayed and unheard.

Some people believed the invention of the phonograph would mean that even fewer people would learn to play music. John Philip Sousa wrote an article for *Appleton's Magazine* in September 1906 entitled "The Menace of Mechanical Music." Sousa predicted that the phonograph would lead to "a marked deterioration in American music and musical taste" and that the amateur musician would disappear.

History seems to have proven Sousa wrong. Rather than discourage people from learning about music, the phonograph seems to have inspired them. The phonograph made it possible for people who had only read about classical composers, or heard one or two pieces performed at a college or in a big city, to hear their works as often as they wished. It also allowed millions more who had never heard of classical music to be exposed to it for the first time. Not long after phonographs appeared, schools began to buy them for use in arts and music courses. Slowly, the interest in classical music grew. Inspired by records by Caruso, Rachmaninoff, Stokowski, and others, more students aspired to careers in classical music than ever before.

The phonograph also changed the way professional musicians approached classical music. Before the phonograph, the small number of classical musicians tended to perform important new works and a few enduring favorites. A vast catalog of exquisite music went unplayed for hundreds of years. Great masters, such as Antonio Vivaldi, Georg Philipp Telemann, Domenico Scarlatti, and Enrico Samartini, were all but forgotten. Even Johann Sebastian Bach was known for just a handful of his works.

Money from the sales of well-known classical records was used to record lesser-known works of equal, and even surpassing, merit. Needing new titles to sell, the record companies supported the revival of many composers whose works lay forgotten in the dusty libraries of Venice, Rome, Vienna, Berlin, Paris, and London. Through records, the great concerti and choral works of Vivaldi lived again. J. S. Bach's sons—Wilhelm Friedemann Bach, Carl Philipp Emanuel Bach, and Johann Christian Bach—became renowned in their own right. Even well-known composers like Franz Joseph Haydn and Wolfgang

The phonograph increased the audience for classical music and enhanced the reputation of long-dead composers like Johann Sebastian Bach.

Amadeus Mozart went through a revival. Their many lesser-known works gained wider listenership, and their popularity rose. Through the power of records, J. S. Bach came to be known as one of classical music's greatest composers.

Broadening Tastes

The phonograph had a similar impact on music even less well known than classical works. Before the phonograph, two indigenous forms of American music, jazz and country, were virtually unknown outside the regions where they arose. Both forms of music had roots in the American South. Jazz evolved in New Orleans from a mixture of African and European traditions. Country music spun off from the hillbilly music of the Appalachian mountain region and the cowboy music of Texas. The first known jazz recordings were "Indiana" and "The Dark Town Strutters Ball," made for the Columbia label around January 30, 1917, by the Original Dixieland Jazz Band led by Dominick (Nick) James La Rocca. Through recordings, both these music forms slowly expanded their influence beyond the regions of their origins. On March 15, 1945, when *Billboard* published its first list of best-selling albums, the number one album was "King Cole Trio," a jazz record featuring Nat King Cole. At one point in 1992, the best-selling album and three of the top ten best-selling albums were by Garth Brooks, a country-western musician.

Easy access to a wide range of music through recordings has led musicians to fuse different styles. A fusion of hillbilly music and a form of jazz known as the blues gave rise to the most popular hy-

An early practitioner of rock-and-roll, Elvis Presley became the most popular solo recording artist of all time.

brid of all to date, rock-and-roll, or rock. Characterized by a strong beat, known as a back beat, rock music quickly became the most popular form of recorded music. One of the early practitioners of rock-and-roll, Elvis Presley, recorded more than 170 major hits between 1956 and 1977, including more than 75 that sold more than a million copies each. Presley also released more than 80 albums, making him the most successful solo recording artist of all time.

Rock music itself has been combined with other forms of music as well. The union of rock and country yielded country rock. A cross between rock and blues created a sound known as soul. Rock has even been combined with classical music to create a hybrid of classical rock.

Rap, one of the most popular forms

Songwriter Paul Simon combined African folk rhythms with his own style of music on his best-selling albums.

of music in the 1990s, is another such hybrid. Its roots go back to the street poetry of the 1970s performed by groups such as the Last Poets. In rap, strongly rhythmic lyrics filled with perfect rhyme are joined with intense percussive music from the rock tradition. The thumping, vibrant sound has inspired young people to create countless new dance steps. Often controversial and sometimes offensive, the lyrics in rap reflect the social tensions felt by young people everywhere, especially those in urban areas.

This list of fusion possibilities is endless. Classical music and jazz music have been combined by flutist Jean-Pierre Rampal and pianist Claude Bolling, among others. The popular songwriter Paul Simon included African folk rhythms and musicians to notable effect in his best-selling albums "Graceland" and "The Rhythm of the Saints." Guitarist Ottmar Liebert has fused jazz and traditional flamenco styles. The Japanese keyboard artist Keiko Matsui blends folk melodies and instruments from her homeland with a contemporary jazz format. Performance artist Laurie Anderson uses everything from cartoon background music to Cajun zydeco dance rhythms in her unusual yet haunting recordings. Such diverse unions, never dreamt of before, have become commonplace because of recorded music.

The revolutions continue today.

Stereo

Impressed by the vast improvements in recorded sound brought about by electronics and vinyl disks, audiophiles coined a new term, high fidelity, to describe the lifelike sound. Played on a high fidelity, or hi-fi, phonograph, the new records reproduced some sounds with near-perfect realism. A single voice, such as that of the poet Dylan Thomas, who made several recordings of his image-rich poetry in the 1950s, came across especially well. So did solo instruments—a solo violin, piano, trumpet, or saxophone.

A high-fidelity phonograph system, or hi-fi, with separate components: turntable, amplifier, and speakers.

Something Lacking

Hi-fi phonographs had limits, however. Recordings of two or more voices or instruments did not sound quite the same on disk as they did in the recording studio. Something was lacking. That something is known as depth.

William S. Bachman, who became the director of engineering for Columbia Records in 1946, described the problem this way:

> The sound produced in the performance of a musical composition is three-dimensional in character. A listener in the same room is able to recognize the direction from which the sound comes . . . by virtue of his two ears. This is because of the small difference of loudness and of arrival time in the two paths between the source of sound and his two ears. It is possible to hear the sound with one ear, but the sense of direction is severely reduced.

For example, if a singer and a pianist are performing side by side, both ears of the listener will perceive both sounds, but slightly differently. The ear nearest the singer will perceive the sound of the singer more strongly than will the ear nearest the piano, and vice-versa. Just as a person's two eyes view the world from slightly different angles and see slightly different things, creating a perception of depth, a person's two ears hear sounds from slightly different angles and register a similar quality of depth. Phonographs with just one

The single speaker that came with most early hi-fi phonographs could not reproduce the deep, rich sounds of a full orchestra. Inventors went to work on this problem and came up with a solution: stereo recording.

speaker could not create the quality of depth, since all the sound came from one point.

The lack of depth was not too noticeable with a single recorded voice or a solo instrument. For example, the sound of a live trumpet solo would come from one point—the end of the horn. A recording of a solo trumpet would also come from one point—the phonograph speaker. The two sounds, the live trumpet and the recorded trumpet, would sound similar. But with a large group, especially an orchestra, the lack of depth was obvious. The sound of a live orchestra would come from many different points. A single speaker of a phonograph could not reproduce such sound realistically.

Two-Channel Sound

To make recorded sound more realistic to human ears, the phonograph had to change. It had to produce sound from two or more locations, and the sound coming from each location had to be different—just as the sounds coming into the two human ears are slightly different. This meant the phonograph had to have at least two speakers. It also meant that when a recording was made, the sound for each speaker had to be recorded through a different microphone. The slight difference in the two recordings would mimic the difference heard by human ears. This process was known as recording in stereo. William Bachman described the process this way:

The magnetic tape recorder converts electric signals from a microphone into magnetic impulses, which are stored on tape. The width of the tape provides enough space to record two separate channels of sound, which can be played back in stereo.

To recreate the original sound field would require a listening room of the same size and shape of the recording studio or concert hall. . . . To attempt to recreate this sound field in a normal living room is an obvious impossibility. It becomes necessary to scale down the size of the source and also the volume level. This is accomplished in stereophonic recording by using fairly large separation of microphones in the recording studio so that the proportions of the original source are maintained by a reduced separation between the loudspeakers in the living room. . . . The fact that two channels are in use preserves the sense of space, the relative location of the instruments, and the direction from which the various sounds originate.

A Threat to the Phonograph

The Ampex Corporation began to make two-channel recordings in 1955. Ampex did not make phonograph records, however. It made recordings on magnetic tape.

This method of sound recording dated back to the hectic summer of 1881, when Alexander Graham Bell, Chichester Bell, and Summer Tainter first tried to record the impression of sound waves using an electromagnet. The first practical system of magnetic recording was invented in 1898 by Valdemar Poulsen of Denmark. Poulsen had recorded the sound vibrations onto pieces of wire. In the 1930s, Fritz Pfleumer of Germany replaced the wire with a length of tape coated with magnetic material. Magnetic tape was the type of recording material used by Ampex.

Ampex made magnetic tapes that carried two separate recordings produced during one recording session. Each of the two recordings was made with a separate microphone. The two microphones were spaced apart in the recording studio to mimic human hearing. The two recordings were placed side by side on the magnetic tape in what were known as tracks. Each of the tracks passed over a sensor known as a head. Each head converted the changing magnetic fields into electrical impulses that played out of a separate speaker. The results were amazing. Two separate channels of sound created the depth that had been missing from single-speaker, or monaural, systems. The two-channel process was known as stereophonic recording, or stereo for short.

Audiophiles were enrapt with the new process. Record company executives could see that the future of their business hinged on the ability to produce stereo records. Or, to put it another way, without stereo, there would be no future. The record companies began a round-the-clock effort to find a way to record two separate channels onto one flat disk.

Two Tracks in One Groove

The most obvious way of doing this was to direct two channels of sound toward two separate styluses and incise two grooves, side by side, on the record. This was similar to Ampex's method of placing two audio tracks side by side on a strip of magnetic tape. The drawback was that a two-groove system would cut in half the amount of sound a disk could hold. A better solution was to fit both channels of sound into one groove. In 1957, two giants of the recording industry—Columbia and Decca Records—were working on just such a system. Before they perfected their design, however, a tiny, almost unheard-of company, the Westrex Company, came up with a solution.

The roots of the Westrex method date back to the very beginning of the phonograph to the different recording techniques of Charles Cros and Thomas Edison. The Westrex researchers saw that it would be possible to combine the two early methods—lateral cut recording and hill-and-dale recording—in one groove. As the recording stylus moved back and forth in response to one channel of sound, it would also move up and down in response to a second. A special two-part pickup stylus would respond to the two incised channels without mixing them. The zig-zag motion of the stylus would send electrical signals down one wire, through the amplifying tubes, to one speaker of the phonograph. At the same time, the up-and-down motion of the stylus would send a different set

A drawing by William Steig decorated the cover of a Columbia Records recording, "Delirium in Hi-Fi." The cartoon illustrates the complex system of components used by phonograph enthusiasts in the 1950s.

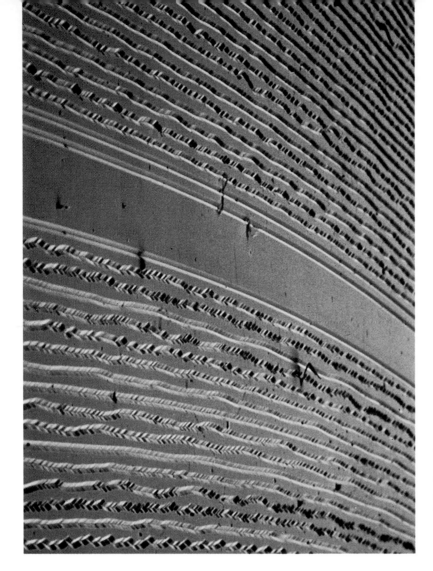

A magnified view of a long playing record shows the concentric grooves that produce sound. The flat space in the middle is the interval between two tracks.

of signals down a second wire, through the tubes, to the second speaker.

Westrex offered to sell rights to their single-groove method to RCA. In the summer of 1957, RCA accepted. The company announced it would begin producing stereo phonographs and single-groove stereo disks as soon as possible.

In the fall of 1957, Columbia and Decca Records revealed their own methods of stereo recording. These systems used a vee-shaped stylus that angled out from the bottom of the lateral-cut groove. One side of the vee lay along one wall of the groove. The other side of the vee touched the opposite wall. Each

side of the vee was wired to a different sound channel in the phonograph. Each wall of the master recording was etched with a similar vee-shaped stylus, so that each wall held a separate recording.

Fearing another battle of competing technologies, like that in the War of the Speeds, industry leaders called upon RCA, Columbia, and Decca to settle on one common method of stereo recording so that all stereo phonographs could play all stereo records. Such an agreement, the leaders said, would benefit both the record companies and the public. The voices of reason prevailed. The three industry giants agreed to share the vee-shaped design. Much work remained to perfect a stereo stylus and phonograph, however.

Home Stereo

Early in 1958, a small company named Audio Fidelity began releasing stereo records made with the Westrex system, even though there were no phonographs capable of producing stereo sound. Stereo disks could be played on hi-fi systems, but the results were not good. The new disks sounded odd— brassy, even tinny. Even so, audiophiles were intrigued.

Within a few weeks, another small company, Fairchild Recording Equipment Company, began selling a stereo stylus to play the new records. Some audiophiles were able to build separate sound channels that lined up with the two-part stylus. Throughout the summer

of 1958, other small companies began selling equipment that would enable record lovers to convert their hi-fi phonographs to stereo. By fall, however, the boom in homemade stereo phonographs came to an end. The major phonograph companies began to offer stereo phonographs, and all the major record companies began to offer stereo disks.

The stereo phonograph was an instant success, although at first it was more of a novelty than anything else. To showcase the new sound system, recording engineers staged elaborate sessions featuring bells, automobile horns, and the sounds of flying aircraft. One disk, produced by Columbia Records, was entitled "Listening in Depth." The album cover gave a detailed account of the workings of stereophonic sound, including close-up photographs of the stereo groove. The selections on the disk were not sound effects, but music. In a pref-

The stereo phonograph was an immediate success. Adults and teenagers alike were captivated by the quality of music they could hear in the comfort of their own homes.

ace printed on the album cover, Goddard Lieberson, president of Columbia Records, wrote:

> No matter what sensations one may experience in stereophonic listening, it is well to remember that the "effects"— the airplanes, trains, and startlingly real "sounds," natural or machine-made— are but momentary pleasures, and that the real value of reproduced sound is furnishing the sublime [grand] experience of music. It is to add to this sublimity that scientists and engineers give so much of their effort—and it is for such use that the new refinement of stereophony is, in the final analysis, eminently worth all of our whiles.

Even so, the selections on "Listening in Depth" were "chosen to illustrate particular aspects of stereophonic sound," according to notes on the album cover. For example, the record includes a version of Duke Ellington's classic composition "Take the A Train." The song begins with the prerecorded sound of a train. The sound moves from one speaker of the phonograph to the other as if the train were passing through the listener's living room.

Music over Novelty

RCA Victor produced a similar record in 1961, entitled "Dynamica, The Sound Your Eyes Can Follow." The album included a brief essay by David Hall, the music editor of *HiFi/Stereo Review*. Like Lieberson, Hall emphasized the importance of music over novelty:

The advent of stereophonic recordings for the home and the equipment on which to play them brought in its wake a whole specialized repertoire of "sound demonstration" discs—recordings which when played on stereo phonographs would provide the hearer with spectacular sonic illusions of motion, directionality and depth. The snarl of racing cars whizzing past the starting line, the New York City subway, a ping-pong game, the bowling alley, the zing of a rifle bullet toward its target, the soft-shoe dance across the stage—these and a host of other novel effects became showpieces for the home stereo listener.

Wonderful as these stereo sound effects may be as aural novelties, they cannot hold the listener's attention for long or over many hearings. The substance of almost all recordings worth living with is, after all—MUSIC.

The RCA Victor recording featured music "chosen on the basis of how well it would lend itself to two-speaker motion." For example, the record begins with Rimsky-Korsakov's classical composition "The Flight of the Bumble Bee." The "Guide to Listening" printed on the album cover states, "Flutist Julius Baker is the 'bee' in the honey of an arrangement. Listen as he flits furiously back and forth between speakers, with the string action following in hot pursuit."

Listeners of these early stereo albums could tell that stereo sound was something entirely new. But they could not imagine how this innovation would be put to use by recording artists to come.

CHAPTER 8

Digital Sound

After the introduction of stereo, the phonograph industry grew as never before. New sales records were set each year, only to be broken the next. Part of this spectacular growth was due to the increase in the populations of the United States, Europe, and Japan after World War II. Children born right after the war grew up to be record-buying teenagers in the late 1950s. At the same time, rock-and-roll music swept across the world like a typhoon, flooding the airwaves and crashing into nearly every home in the industrialized world. The sales of phonographs and records rose with the tide.

At the same time stereo music exploded onto the scene, another new invention was quietly making historic inroads of its own. That machine was the computer. Its information storage and retrieval systems proved to be of great value to large companies that kept extensive records of sales, inventory, and accounting. The speed with which it performed its tasks made the computer especially valuable to companies in quickly changing markets. It was perfect

Population growth in the industrialized nations after World War II and the popularity of rock-and-roll pushed record sales to new heights in the 1960s and 1970s. This record store is crowded with records for young listeners.

for the recording industry. Record companies used the new machines to track sales and control the distribution of its fast-selling music. It did not take long for the new technology to work its way into the recording of music itself.

Computers and Music

In the mid-1960s, studio engineers began using computers to record and refine music. The way computers did this was unlike any other method of recording sound.

Every other recording medium—from Cros's lateral-cut groove to Ampex's magnetic tape—stored sound in a three-dimensional, physical form. The squiggles on Léon Scott's coated paper, the dimples in Edison's tinfoil, the zigzag grooves in Tainter's wax cylinder, even the magnetically arranged particles on the surface of magnetic tape—each of these was a physical copy, or analog, of the original sound waves that formed them. If a sound wave was gently rounded, its physical record—the dimple, lateral cut, or magnetic impression—also was gently rounded. If the sound wave was jagged, its analog was jagged. The stored sound was reproduced when another physical object, such as a stylus or magnetic tape head, came into contact with the analog.

The computer made a record of sound waves, too, but this record was not physical. It was informational. Sound entered the computer in a physical form, but the computer recorded its impression as a series of numbers. The physical impression was not saved. The numbers were.

The process of assigning a numerical value to a sound wave was called pulse code modulation, or PCM. Developed by NHK Technical Research of Great Britain, PCM was given its first public demonstration in 1967. The theory behind the new process was not new however. In fact, it had been described thirty-nine years earlier by an American scientist named Harry Nyquist.

Nyquist knew that the range of human hearing was between 20 vibrations per second on the low end to 20,000 vibrations per second on the high end. He also knew that each sound wave had a high point, known as a peak, and a low point, known as a valley. It occurred to Nyquist that one way to record sound would be to measure, or sample, sound waves many times each second. Since the shortest sound wave lasts only 1/20,000 of a second, Nyquist reasoned, the recording device would have to be able to sample the sound at least 20,000 times a second. To get a true picture of the entire sound wave—its peak and its valley—each sound wave would have to be sampled at least twice. The best sampling rate, Nyquist concluded, was not 20,000 times a second, but 40,000 times a second.

Nyquist published his findings, or theorem, in 1928. The world scarcely noticed. Although his theory made sense, no device existed that could possibly sample a sound wave so often. Even if one did, how would the information be stored? What could be used to retrieve it? The whole notion was so impractical that it seemed absurd.

Storing Digits

Twenty years later, Nyquist's concept made a little more sense. In 1943, the U.S. Navy developed the first computer.

The computer used electrical impulses to store and process numbers. The presence of electrical current stood for the number "one." The absence of current stood for the number "zero." Larger numbers were represented by a series of ones and zeros. Since this numbering system used only two numbers, it was named binary code. Each digit in the binary code was called a bit, short for binary digit. Since an electrical current can be switched on and off thousands of times a second, a computer could process numbers very quickly—fast enough to sample sound waves at the speed Nyquist described and to store the results.

In 1948, a British scientist named C. E. Shannon described how to use a computer to measure and record sound waves. He called his process pulse code modulation (PCM). Since PCM assigned digits to the changes, or modulation, of sound waves, it also became known as digital recording, or digitizing.

Converting Sound into Numbers

Once again, however, theory had raced ahead of technology. No device existed to put Shannon's ideas into practice until NHK Technical Research built one in 1967. The NHK device measured the loudness, or amplitude, of a sound wave on a scale between 0 (silence) and 65,535 (extreme loudness). This measuring system was known as quantization. A device known as an analog-to-digital converter (ADC) assigned one of the 65,536 digits (including zero) to a sound wave every 1/44,100 of a second. Instead of recording sound as a continuous wave, PCM recorded it as millions of separate points. Instead of painting sound, as an analog system did, PCM built a mosaic.

To reproduce sound, the digital system used a device known as a digital-to-analog converter (DAC). This device changed the digital data into something that could be heard. It turned digits into pulses of electricity that could move through a stereo system. These pulses caused the speakers to vibrate, creating sound. The digital system performed this task with great precision. A wave form that registered 21,055 as it entered the ADC came out of the DAC at 21,055 as well. The pulse of electricity created by the DAC conformed to this number, causing the speaker to vibrate at precisely the right speed.

In the 1960s, PCM devices began to be used in the recording industry to

A sound technician in a digital recording studio adjusts his equipment. Digital recording made it easier for record companies to combine, edit, and clean up musical performance.

make master recording tapes. Digital recording had an advantage over analog sound. The digital information could be changed at will. For example, if something did not sound good, the sound engineer could locate the problem section of the tape with a computer and change its numerical value. In this way, digital masters could be "cleaned up" before they were used to make records and tapes.

Limitless Range

Digital tapes also sounded much better than analog tapes. The reason, again, was that digital recording did not have the physical limits that burdened analog systems. Even with the most sensitive analog system, the device that made the physical impression could only move so far in a given period of time. The digital system did not have this physical limitation. The values of the digits could change as much as needed every 1/40,000 of a second. Nothing in the PCM system had to move from one place to another to record a sound. Each sample taken by the device was just a number. That number could be anything from 0 through 65,536. The next number recorded by the system could also be anywhere within the same range—near the previous number or far away. A digital system could respond more quickly to changes in sounds than an analog system could.

Because it assigned forty thousand numerical values to sound waves every second, a PCM recording system had to store an enormous number of digits. This is why NHK Technical Researchers used one-inch videotape for recording

rather than one-half-inch audio tape or the one-quarter-inch tape used in the popular magnetic tapes known as cassettes. A cassette tape could scarcely hold enough PCM data for even one song, let alone an entire album. A one-inch tape could hold the information, but it was bulky and therefore difficult to handle and store.

Optical Storage

In 1969, the European electronics firm Philips began working on a method of storing digital data in a more compact format. The medium that showed the most promise was known as an optical

Musical recordings could be mixed and edited to eliminate problem areas and improve sound quality.

storage disk. As the name suggests, the optical storage disk recorded digits in a visual format. Binary code digits stored on magnetic tape caused a laser gun to fire pulses of laser light at the surface of a glass disk coated with light-sensitive chemicals. Each time the laser fired, it made a small indentation, or pit, in the surface of the disk. Each pit represented the number zero. When the laser did not fire, it left a flat area, or flat, on the surface of the disk. The flats represented the number one. The combination of ones and zeros corresponded to the digits stored on the master magnetic tape.

Once they had etched a glass master disk, researchers at Philips coated its surface with a silver and nickel alloy. The metal coating made a reverse impression of the flats and pits on the disk. The coating was separated from the glass master and used as a mold to make even stronger metal disks. These disks were used to stamp the impression onto plastic disks coated with a layer of shiny aluminum just 1/4 of a millionth of an inch thick. The aluminum was then sealed under a protective layer of clear plastic.

The shiny surface of an optical storage disk is encoded with digital information. The surface is scanned by a laser beam, and the reflections are "read" by a light-sensitive component attached to a computer.

Laser Light

To read the information on the plastic disk, the Philips researchers used a device known as a laser scanner. The laser scanner aimed a narrow beam of laser light through the plastic and onto the shiny surface. When the light struck a flat, its flat surface reflected the beam back toward its source, known as a beam splitter. The light passed through the beam splitter to a light-sensitive device known as a photodiode. The photo-

diode converted the pulse of light into a pulse of electricity. This pulse corresponded to the digit one. When the laser light struck a pit, the indented surface reflected the beam at an angle. This light did not reach the photodiode, so it registered a zero.

The Compact Disc

Philips was the first company to develop an optical storage system, but it was not the only one. RCA, Pioneer, Thomson, JVC, and Sony were developing systems as well. As the electronics companies began to look into using optical storage for music disks, they realized that they could all sell more disks if they devised

HOW COMPACT DISCS ARE MADE

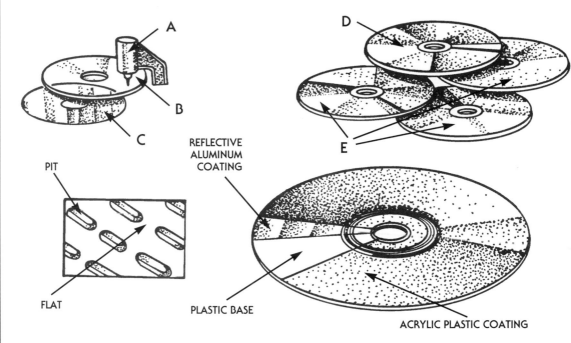

A

D

B

C

E

REFLECTIVE
ALUMINUM
COATING

PIT

FLAT

PLASTIC BASE

ACRYLIC PLASTIC COATING

Compact discs are called digital recordings because they contain a digital, or numerical, record of sound waves. In this way, compact discs differ from vinyl phonograph records, which contain a three-dimensional record of sound waves, known as an analog.

During a digital recording session a computer measures the electric current generated by sound waves and stores the measurements in a numerical code, called binary code, on a digital master tape. The information on the master tape is fed into a computer-controlled laser engraver (A). Each time the computer reads a "zero" on the tape, it triggers the engraver to fire a laser beam at a rotating glass disc (B). The disc is coated with light-sensitive chemicals. The pulses of laser light dissolve portions of the chemical coating, leaving tiny pits in the surface of the glass disc. Each pit represents the number "zero" while the

spaces between the pits, known as flats, represent the number "one."

The glass disc is coated with silver and nickel (C). The coating is removed from the glass disc and used as a mold to form stronger metal discs (D). These discs are reverse (negative) copies of the original. Where the glass disc had pits, for example, the metal copy has raised points. Thousands of plastic discs (E) are then stamped from these negative copies. The plastic discs are exact (positive) copies of the original glass disc.

The plastic discs are coated with a layer of aluminum only 1/4 of a millionth of an inch thick. The aluminum coating reflects the light from the compact disc player's laser scanner so that the player can "read" the digits encoded on the disc. In the final step, the shiny discs are then coated with a layer of clear acrylic plastic to protect the aluminum surface.

a common format, as the phonograph companies had at the advent of stereo. In 1980, the leaders of Philips, Sony, and Polygram Records announced a common set of standards for optical audio disks. In 1981, thirty-five electronics companies agreed to follow the standards. They even agreed on a name for the new devices: compact discs, or CDs.

Because they reproduced sound in an entirely different way, CDs could not be played on a traditional phonograph. A new machine—in essence, a new form of phonograph—was needed.

In October 1982, Philips, Sony, and CBS offered this new form of phonograph—the compact disc player—for sale. The world's first compact disc, Billy Joel's "52nd Street," was also released.

In the first full year of sales, only 35,000 compact disc players were sold worldwide. Most of these were purchased by music professionals and audiophiles. The general public remained skeptical about the new systems. Other sound systems—magnetic tape cartridges that played a continuous loop of tape recorded with four or eight tracks of music, for example—had arrived with great fanfare only to be replaced by something better a couple of years later. Perhaps the same would happen with the compact disc. Besides, the new players and discs were expensive. Compact discs cost from 25 percent to 50 percent more than vinyl phonograph records.

Launching an Industry

Industry leaders recognized the problem right away, and they decided to do something about it. In 1983, representatives from the record companies and the

manufacturers of CD players, discs, and recording equipment formed the Compact Disc Group. The goal of this association was to help the new technology gain wider acceptance. The Compact Disc Group held a series of meetings in which members were encouraged to speak out about any and all problems associated with CDs. The group discussed everything from the lack of titles available on CD to the type of packaging used to encase the shiny discs.

One major problem with the early systems was in the tracking of the rings of pits and flats. Since the laser scanner was aiming at such a small target, it was

Billy Joel's "52nd Street" was the first recording released on compact disc.

To bring digital sound into the home, electronics companies invented a new kind of phonograph— the compact disc player.

The Compact Disc Group knew that if more people actually heard the systems, they would want to buy them. The group encouraged the manufacturers to offer free players to be given away as prizes. It convinced department stores to demonstrate the machines. It encouraged record stores to use the new machines in their sound systems. Knowing how important radio was in shaping music buying patterns, the Compact Disc Group spent a great deal of time promoting the technology to radio stations.

Fast Growth

The strategy worked. On the one hand, the makers of the equipment quickly identified problems with the machines and corrected them. They also made more affordable systems. At the same time, more and more people heard the new systems for themselves. Radio stations adopted CD technology very quickly. Soon, some radio stations advertised that they played only CD music. The skepticism began to fade.

The Christmas season of 1985 was a turning point for CD technology. Consumers put aside their fears and bought the new gadgets in record numbers. Many stores sold out of certain players. Disc sales took off.

By 1990, the manufacturers of CD players were selling 9 million units a year. Disc sales climbed from the 800,000 sold in 1983 to more than 286 million. The CD had arrived.

By the middle of the 1980s, many new records were being released only on CD and cassette tape, not vinyl. Just as LPs had replaced the 78s that had been the foundation of the recording industry, CDs began to replace LPs.

easy for the device to slip off track. This was especially true in portable players—hand-held boom boxes and car stereo systems. Members of the Compact Disc Group worked together to solve these and other problems.

The secret weapon of the Compact Disc Group was the product itself. Its sound was nearly flawless. Since the only thing touching the CD was laser light, the system produced no surface noise. Digital sound erupts out of pure silence, just as in a sound studio. Because of the digital encoding, the range of sound was greater than with analog systems. The highs were higher, the lows were lower, and complex wave forms came across with clarity.

HOW A COMPACT DISC PLAYER WORKS

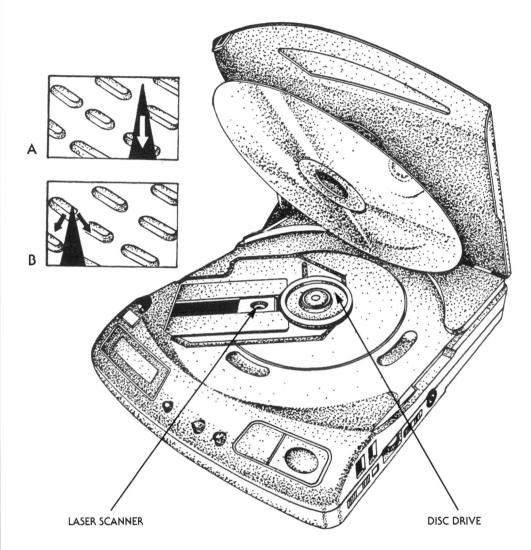

LASER SCANNER

DISC DRIVE

The disk drive of a compact disc player spins the disc at a rate up to 500 revolutions per minute. The laser scanner focuses a laser beam onto the shiny underside of the compact disc. The smooth area of the disc, known as a flat, reflects the light back to the laser scanner (A). The laser scanner converts the flash of light into an electrical pulse. The computer in the compact disc player reads the electrical pulse as a "one." The indented portions of the disc, known as pits, reflect the beam at an angle, so it is not read by the laser scanner (B). The computer in the compact disc player reads the absence of an electrical pulse as a "zero." The compact disc player converts these numbers into electric signals causing the loudspeaker to vibrate, producing sound.

Doubts About CDs

Not everyone was enthralled with the new technology, however. Some audiophiles disputed the idea that CDs were superior to LPs. The problem, according to these experts, is that by breaking sound waves into thousands of tiny pieces, digital recording destroys the fluid beauty of sound. It does not matter how often the digital system samples a sound wave, it still only records pieces of it—the mosaic rather than the paint-

Smaller and easier to handle than a vinyl record, the compact disc holds as much music on one side as the LP does on two.

ing. Between these pieces, the critics point out, is a total absence of sound—utter silence. Although a listener cannot hear these silences consciously, his or her brain perceives them on a subconscious level.

This perception, say the critics, creates a feeling of unease. According to this view, digital recordings lack the warmth of natural sound. They inspire a kind of unconscious shiver. Analog impressions, on the other hand, are continuous, like sound itself. They create feelings of warmth and well-being.

Despite their claims, the vinyl enthusiasts are a tiny minority. For most people, the lack of surface noise alone makes CDs more pleasant to listen to than vinyl records. In addition, CDs are easy to handle and play. They hold the entire recording on one side, so they do not have to be turned over. Because the laser can be directed to any portion of the recording at any time, the CD listener can switch to any selection on the CD at any time. The listener can repeat a selection as often as desired and even program the player to play the selections in a certain order. The fact that CDs almost never wear out makes their somewhat high price seem like more of a bargain.

Smaller Formats

Despite its advantages, the 4¾-inch compact disc is not the final form sound recordings will take. Already, Sony offers a Mini Disc, or MD, that is just 2½-inches across, yet holds seventy-four minutes of music—about the same as a CD. The tiny discs use a combination of optical and magnetic technology to store sound. The magnetic technology

Sony's Mini Disc player is the size of a hand-held camera. The discs are just 2 ½ inches across but hold seventy-four minutes of music, which is about the same as a compact disc.

means that, unlike traditional CDs, which only play prerecorded music, Mini Discs can be used to both make and play recordings. The portable Mini Disc player, which is about the size of a hand-held camera, can be carried anywhere. Its designers included a computer microchip in it to store about three seconds of music while the device is playing. The three seconds of storage allows the player to keep playing even when the laser scanner is knocked off the recording track by a sudden bump.

Further miniaturization will continue to be the trend for sound systems.

Someday, computer microchips themselves may be encoded with enough digital information to store not just three seconds worth of music, but an entire song, an album, or even an opera. Such a tiny storage device would require a small player. Perhaps the entire system could be fitted to the ear, like a hearing aid or even an earring. Deep within the high-tech jewel, the music of great recording artists—from Enrico Caruso to Laurie Anderson—will continue to play, enchanting humankind with the beauty of sound.

Glossary

■ ■

amplify: To increase strength.

analog-to-digital converter (ADC): A device for measuring physical motion in digital units.

audiophile: An enthusiast of high-quality sound reproduction.

aural: Pertaining to the ear or the sense of hearing.

binary code: A numerical system in which any number can be expressed as 0 or 1 or a combination of these digits.

bit: A unit of information, short for binary digit.

centrifugal force: The inertial reaction by which a body moves away from a center around which it revolves.

diaphragm: A flexible membrane or partition.

dictaphone: A device that records and reproduces speech.

digital-to-analog converter (DAC): A device for converting information stored as digits into electrical pulses that cause a loudspeaker to vibrate.

electromagnet: A device in which a core of soft iron becomes a magnet when an electric current passes through a coil of wire surrounding it.

electroplate: The process of coating objects with metal using electricity.

elocution: The art of public speaking.

flat: The flat portion of a compact disc, signifying the number 1 in binary code.

flywheel: A wheel heavy enough to resist sudden changes of speed, used to secure uniform motion in the working parts of a machine.

graphophone: An early type of phonograph developed by the members of the Volta Laboratory.

high fidelity: The reproduction of a signal or a sound with a minimum of distortion; also called hi-fi.

incise: To cut into with a sharp instrument.

indent: To press or push in so as to form a dent or depression; impress.

laser: A device that can generate light waves of a specific frequency.

lateral: Pertaining to the side or sides; situated at, occurring, or coming from the side.

mechanical: Of, involving, or having to do with the construction, operation, or design of a machine.

monaural: A system of sound reproduction in which the sound is perceived as coming from one direction only; distinguished from stereophonic.

optics: The study of light and vision.

patent: Government protection given to an inventor, securing for a specific time the exclusive right to manufacture, exploit, use, and sell an invention.

phonautograph: A device for recording the presence and shape of sound waves.

phonograph: A device for recording and reproducing sound.

photodiode: A device that converts light waves into electricity.

pickup: A crystal, ceramic, or magnetic device that converts the movement of a needle in a record groove into electrical impulses.

pit: A dent or depression in the surface of a compact disc, signifying the number 0 in binary code.

pulse code modulation (PCM): The process of recording sound by assigning numerical values to portions of each sound wave.

shellac: A varnishlike solution containing flake shellac.

sibilant: Denoting those consonants produced by the passage of breath through a narrow opening, as (s), (sh), and (th).

stearine: A solid form of fat.

stereo: A stereophonic system.

stereophonic: A system of sound reproduction in which two or more loudspeakers are placed to give the effect of hearing the sound from more than one direction; distinguished from monaural.

stylus: A pointed instrument for marking or engraving; also the needle of a phonograph; also called a style.

turntable: The rotating disk that carries a phonograph record.

vacuum tube: An electron tube having a vacuum within its envelope and a method of heating a cathode to stimulate electron emission.

vibration: A periodic, usually rapid motion of an object.

For Further Reading

Dorothy Harley Eber, *Genius at Work, Images of Alexander Graham Bell.* New York: The Viking Press, 1982.

David C. Knight, *The First Book of Sound.* New York: Franklin Watts, Inc., 1960.

Barbara Mitchell, *The Wizard of Sound, a Story About Thomas Edison.* Minneapolis: Carolrhoda Books, Inc., 1991.

Elizabeth Rider Montgomery, *Alexander Graham Bell, Man of Sound.* Champaign, Illinois: Garrard Publishing Company, 1963.

Works Consulted

■■

Bryan Brewer and Edd Key, *The Compact Disc Book*. San Diego: Harcourt Brace Jovanovich, 1987.

Robert V. Bruce, *Bell: Alexander Graham Bell and the Conquest of Solitude*. Boston: Little, Brown, 1973.

Roland Gelatt, *The Fabulous Phonograph*. New York: Lippincott, 1955.

Philip W. Goetz, ed., *The New Encyclopaedia Britannica*. Chicago: Encyclopaedia Britannica, 1987.

Otto Johnson, ed., *Information Please Almanac*. Boston: Houghton Mifflin Company, 1992.

Donald McFarlan, ed., *The Guinness Book of World Records 1992*. New York: Bantam Books, 1992.

Oliver Read and Walter L. Welch, *From Tin Foil to Stereo, Evolution of the Phonograph*. Indianapolis: Howard W. Sams & Co., Inc., 1976.

James Robert Smart, *A Wonderful Invention: A Brief History of the Phonograph from Tinfoil to the LP*. Washington D.C.: Library of Congress, 1977.

Index

Academy of Sciences in Paris, 17, 25
Amden, James L., 39
American Graphophone Company, 34, 37
Ampex Corporation
  magnetic stereo tapes, 10, 70, 71, 76
analog-to-digital converter (ADC), 77
Anderson, Laurie, 67, 85
Anglo Italian Commerce Company, 49
Audio Fidelity, stereo records, 73
Audion (vacuum tube), 50

Bach, Carl Philipp Emanuel, 65
Bach, Johann Christian, 65
Bach, Johann Sebastian, 65, 66
Bach, Wilhelm Friedemann, 65
Bachman, William S., 68, 69-70
Batchelor, Charles, 18-19, 20
Beatles, The, 10, 63
Beethoven, Ludwig van, 64
Bell, Alexander Graham
  builds phonautograph, 13, 14
  Edison and, 28, 35
  ideas for the phonograph, 28-29
  improvements to phonograph, 31-33
  invention of the telephone, 27-28
  magnetic recording experiments, 70
  research laboratory of, 30
  telephone companies and, 17
Bell, Chichester, 70
  improvements to phonograph, 30-34
Bell Telephone Company
  research with electricity and recording, 51
Berlin, Irving, 62
Berliner, Emile
  work on record disk, 10, 42-46, 56
Bettini, Gianni, 47
Billboard magazine
  list of best-selling records, 63, 66
blues music, 66
Bolling, Claude, 67
British Berliner Gramophone Company, 49
British Gramophone Company, 51
Brooks, Garth, 66
Bruce, Robert V., 28

Caruso, Enrico, 65, 85
  first recordings of, 48-49, 62
cassette tapes, 78
classical music

effect of phonograph on, 64-66
  first records, 48-49
classical rock, 66
Clemens, Samuel, 47
Cole, Nat King, 66
Columbia Phonograph Company, 41, 47-49
  use of electricity in recording, 51, 54
Columbia Records
  long playing records (LP), 11, 55-56
  work on stereo records, 71, 72, 73-74
Compact Disc Group, 81-82
compact discs (CDs), 11
  advantages of, 82, 84
  how they are made, 79-80
  Mini Disc (MD), 11, 84
  players for, 81-83
  problems with, 81-82, 84
composers
  effect of recording industry on, 62-67
computers
  development of, 75, 76-77
  recording of music with, 76-79, 84
Conreid, Heinrich, 49
country-western music
  effect of phonograph on, 58-59, 66
country rock, 66
Cros, Charles
  as a poet, 12
  Edison's phonograph and, 24-25
  ideas to improve recording, 31
  method for recording and reproducing sound,
    10, 15-17, 43, 44, 71
  scientific interests of, 12
Crosby, Bing, 10, 57, 62

Decca Records
  work on stereo records, 71, 72
De Forest, Lee
  invention of Audion, 50
dictaphone
  invention of, 35-36
digital recording, 77-79
digital-to-analog converter (DAC), 77
disc jockeys, 59-60
dolls, talking, 26, 27

ear, human
  how it works, 12, 13, 68-69
Edison, Thomas Alva

builds a talking machine, 17
opinion of gramophone, 45
phonograph and
  improvements to, 29, 35-36, 71
  invention of, 10, 19-23
  marketing of, 26-27, 30, 36-37
  patents for, 24-25
research laboratory of, 18-19
rivalry with Alexander Graham Bell, 28, 35
stock ticker improvements, 18
telegraph improvements, 20, 21
telephone and, 20, 35
work on copying recordings, 39
Edison Speaking Phonograph Company, 29, 30, 35, 37
electricity
  used to improve phonograph recordings, 51-53
  use in radio technology, 50
Ellington, Duke, 63, 73
Ellis, Alexander, 30

Fairchild Recording Equipment Company, 73
Foster, Stephen, 62, 63
Franklin Institute, 45

Gaisberg, Fred, 49
Gershwin, George, 63
Glass, Louis, 38
Gluck, Alma, 62
gramophone, 45-51
graphophone, 32-38
Guest, Lionel, 10, 51

Haydn, Franz Joseph, 65
hearing
  how the ear works, 12, 13, 68-69
high fidelity (hi-fi), 68, 73
Holiday, Billie, 63
Hubbard, Gardiner, 28, 30

International Zonophone Company, 49

jazz music
  effect of phonograph on, 49, 58, 66
Joel, Billy, 81
Johnson, Edward H., 21, 24
Johnson, Eldridge, 46-48
Jolson, Al, 49
Jones, Joseph W.

patent on wax records, 47-48
JVC
  optical disks, 79

Kris Kross, 10
Kruesi, John, 18, 21

Last Poets, 67
Lennon, John, 63
Leoncavallo, Ruggiero, 49
Library of Congress, 11
Lieberson, Goddard, 74
Liebert, Ottmar, 67
Lippincott, Jesse, 37-39
loudspeaker, 50

magnetic recording, 70, 71, 76, 78
Marconi, Guglielmo, 50
Matsui, Keiko, 67
Merriman, H.O., 10, 51
Metropolitan Opera Company, 49
Miller, Glenn, 57, 62, 63
Mozart, Wolfgang Amadeus, 65-66
music
  first phonograph records of, 39-42
  types of
    blues, 66
    classical
      effect of phonograph on, 64-66
      first records, 48-49
    classical rock, 66
    country-western
      effect of phonograph on, 58-59, 66
    country rock, 66
    fusion of, 66
    jazz
      effect of phonograph on, 49, 58, 66
    popular
      effect of phonograph on, 62-63
      first records, 48-49, 57
    rap, 66-67
    rock-and-roll, 66, 75
    soul, 66
musicians
  effect of recording industry on, 62-67

National Phonograph Company, 54
New England Phonograph Company, 47
New Jersey Phonograph Company, 47

NHK Technical Research of Great Britain digital
  recording and, 11, 76, 77, 78
North American Phonograph Company, 37, 39
Nyquist, Harry
  sound wave research, 76-77

Ohio Phonograph Company, 39
opera, 48-49, 64
orchestras
  early difficulty of recording, 42, 53, 69
Original Dixieland Jazz Band, 66
Orthophonic Victrola, 54

Pacific Coast Phonograph Company, 38
Paderewski, Ignacy Jan, 48
payola, 59-60
Pfleumer, F., 70
Philips
  optical disks, 10, 78-79, 81
phonautograph
  invention of, 12-14, 44
  used to record and reproduce sound, 15-17
phonograph
  business uses for, 34, 35, 37
  changes the music industry, 62-67
  coin-operated machines, 38
  compact disc players, 81, 83
  early ideas for, 27, 28
  early problems with, 30, 42
  Edison invents, 10, 19-23
    how it worked, 21-23
    improvements on, 29
  electric, 52-55, 57
  entertainment uses, 38, 41, 48-49, 58-67
    impact on radio, 59-60, 62
  high fidelity (hi-fi), 68, 73
  stereo, 73-74
  Tainter and Bells improve, 31-33
photoengraving
  principles used in recording sound, 15-16
Pioneer optical disks, 79
Porter, Cole, 63
Poulsen, Valdemar, 70
Presley, Elvis, 66
pulse code modulation (PCM), 76-77, 78

Rachmaninoff, Sergey, 48, 65
radio
  early technology, 50-51

first commercials, 58
impact on phonographs, 58-60, 62
use of compact disc technology, 82
Rampal, Jean-Pierre, 67
rap music, 66-67
RCA Victor
  creates 45-rpm records, 11, 56-57
  creates long playing records, 11, 55, 56
  "gold record" awards, 62
  optical disks, 79
  stereo phonographs, 72
  stereo records, 74
recording industry
  beginnings of, 39-40
  changes field of music, 62-67
  disks improve business, 46-47
  early drawbacks of, 42
recording methods
  analog, 76, 78, 84
  compact disc, 79-81
  digital, 77-79, 84
  stereo, 69-71
  tape, 70, 71, 76, 78
records
  acoustic recordings, 48-49
  artists
    Caruso's *Vesti la giubba*, 49, 62
    Cole's "King Cole Trio," 66
    Crosby's "White Christmas," 62
    Foster's "I Dream of Jeannie with the Light
      Brown Hair," 63
    Gluck's "Carry Me Back to Old Virginny," 62
    Joel's "52nd Street," 81
    La Rocca's "Indiana" & "The Dark Town
      Strutters' Ball," 66
    Miller's "Chattanooga Choo Choo," 62, 63
    Simon's "Graceland" and "The Rhythm of
      the Saints," 67
  Billboard's best-selling records, 63, 66
  copies sold, 62, 66, 75
  electricity improves quality, 51-53
  materials used, 10
    aluminum, 79-80
    glass, 79-80
    metal, 15-16, 44
    paper, 20-21
    rubber, 45
    shellac, 46-48
    tape, 70-71, 76-78

tinfoil, 21-23, 30
vinyl, 56
wax, 31, 35-36, 47-48
music industry changed by, 62-67
music styles
classical, 48-49, 64-66
country-western, 58-59, 66
jazz, 49, 58, 66
popular, 48-49, 57, 62
types of
45-rpm recordings, 11, 56-57
cylinders, 23, 29, 31-33, 35, 44-45, 54
disks
how they are made, 61
improvements in, 47-48
invention of, 43-46
long playing (LP), 10, 55-56, 82
stereo, 71-74
Rimsky-Korsakov, Nikolay, 74
rock-and-roll music, 66, 75
Rodgers, Richard, 63

Samartini, Enrico, 65
Scarlatti, Domenico, 65
Scientific American, 21, 24
Scott, Léon, 43
invents phonautograph, 10, 12-14, 20, 44
Shannon, C.E., 77
Simon, Paul, 67
Sinatra, Frank, 57
Smart, James Robert, 49
Smith, Bessie, 49, 58
Smithsonian Institution, 32, 33
Sondheim, Stephen, 63
Sony
optical disks, 11, 79, 81, 84
sound waves
first record of, 12-14
pulse code modulation (PCM), 76-77, 78
Sousa, John Philip
first recording star, 41-42, 47
opposition to the phonograph, 64

stereo recording, 69-71
Stokowski, Leopold
first recordings of, 48, 65

Tainter, Charles Sumner, 30, 47, 70
improvements to phonograph, 31-33
talking books, 11
tape recordings, 70, 71, 76, 78
Telemann, Georg Philipp, 65
telephone
Edison and, 20, 35, 43
invention of, 27-28, 43
patent for, 28
refinements to, 50
Thomas, Dylan, 68
Thomson optical disks, 79

U.S. Gramophone Company, 45
U.S. Navy
first computer and, 76-77

vacuum tubes
use in phonographs, 51
Victor Company
electric phonograph, 54
Victor Talking Machine Company, 48, 49
uses electricity to record, 51, 54
see also RCA Victor
Vivaldi, Antonio, 65
Volta Graphophone Company, 34
Volta Laboratory
formation of, 30
improvements in phonograph, 31-33
patents for phonograph, 33-34

Watson, Thomas, 28-29
Western Union
stock ticker and, 18
telephone patent and, 28
Westrex Company
creates stereo records, 71-72, 73
Williams, Hank, 63

About the Author

The author of nine books for young people, Bradley Steffens first thought about becoming a writer when his high school creative writing teacher, James Malone, read one of his poems aloud to the class. At the time, Steffens dreamed of being a poet and songwriter like his hero, John Lennon. Since then, Steffens has won several prizes for his poetry and seen more than fifty of his poems published. He also has written dozens of songs by himself and with various collaborators. Although a few of these songs have been published, none has yet appeared on a phonograph record or compact disc.

Picture Credits

■■■